Ivan Turgenev

TURGENEV IN ENGLISH

A Checklist of Works by and about Him

Compiled by
RISSA YACHNIN *and* DAVID H. STAM

With an Introductory Essay by
MARC SLONIM

Upsala College
Library
East Orange, N. J.

New York
The New York Public Library
1962

THIS VOLUME HAS BEEN PUBLISHED WITH HELP
FROM THE EMILY ELLSWORTH FORD SKEEL FUND

* * *

Library of Congress Catalog Card Number: 61–11067

Printed at The New York Public Library
form p692 [11-2-62 1m]

Preface

THIS checklist was originally intended as a tribute to the memory of Ivan Sergeyevich Turgenev (1818–1883) on the seventy-fifth anniversary of his death. The first section takes account of all works by Turgenev published in English translation, including collected editions, selections, and individually published works. The collected editions are arranged chronologically while the selections and individually published works are arranged alphabetically by English title. A second section lists stories, prose poems, and other works of Turgenev which were published in anthologies and periodicals. These are arranged alphabetically by the titles under which they were published, with individual stories and prose poems from *A Sportsman's Notebook* and *Poems in Prose* being brought together under those titles. The checklist concludes with a large section dealing with Turgenev criticism in English, arranged chronologically.

Encyclopedia entries, brief notes, theatrical notices, adaptations from Turgenev, and other trivia have as a rule not been included. No special effort has been made to locate book reviews published after 1904, when publication of the Hapgood translation of the collected works was completed. Book reviews published before that time have been included as separate entries in the chronological listing of Turgenev criticism, thus giving an approximate idea of the progress of Turgenev studies in the nineteenth-century Anglo-Saxon world.

Most entries have been personally examined. In addition to checking entries for Turgenev in the *National Union Catalog* and in the printed catalogs of the Library of Congress, the Slavonic Division of The New York Public Library, and the British Museum, the compilers have also searched through the collections of Princeton, Harvard, and Columbia universities.

Much difficulty was encountered in arriving at a satisfactory listing of the collected editions of Turgenev's works, especially of the Garnett and Hapgood translations. These were published piecemeal as well as complete and the more popular volumes were frequently reissued, printed from the same plates. We have had to be content with listing the first publication of each volume in the collected editions, the dates in which complete sets were reprinted, and then listing whatever separate reprints we have found to exist. Presumably there are several more.

Stories published in periodicals often appeared under very non-Turgenevian titles; as much as possible these have been traced to the more standard English titles and so noted.

The index includes an alphabetical list of authors and translators, and an index of titles containing the transliterated Russian titles and the translated titles of all works listed in this checklist. All title variations of a translated work are listed in this index under the Russian title (e. g. for *Liza* etc see *Dvoryanskoye gnezdo*). For variant titles of a work for which only one English title is known, bracketed reference is made after each English title to the transliterated Russian title.

The compilers are grateful to Marc Slonim for contributing the introductory essay and to Richard C. Lewanski for his friendly encouragement. The compilers are also indebted to the work of Royal A. Gettmann, whose *Turgenev in England and America* (Univ of Illinois 1941; item 416) critically charted much of the material published before 1936.

R. Y.
D. S.

Table of Contents

PREFACE   5

TURGENEV REVISITED   9

WORKS BY TURGENEV:

   COLLECTED WORKS:

      Collected editions   17

      Selected Stories and Plays   20

   SEPARATELY PUBLISHED WORKS   21

   ARTICLES, STORIES, AND POEMS PUBLISHED IN ANTHOLOGIES
      AND PERIODICALS   25

WORKS ABOUT TURGENEV   33

TITLE INDEX   43

AUTHOR AND TRANSLATOR INDEX   53

Turgenev Revisited

A HUNDRED YEARS ago, in 1855, the first translations from Turgenev's *Sportsman's Sketches* appeared in French and British periodicals, and since that time his works have continued to gain an ever increasing acclaim in the Western world. Henry James, one of his fervent admirers, was not exaggerating when he wrote in 1874 that the Russian was "the first novelist of the day," and Howells confessed a few years later that he had formed for Turgenev "one of the profoundest literary passions" of his life. At the beginning of the present century Arnold Bennett, asked to name the twelve best novels of world literature, included six of Turgenev's in his honor list. Flaubert and Galsworthy, Conrad and Maupassant paid high tribute to Turgenev and ranked him with Fielding, Thackeray, and Balzac.

Turgenev was the first Russian writer to conquer large audiences outside his native land. He actually introduced Russian literature to Europe and America which, through him, discovered and admired the originality of Russian genius. The impact of his own work, moreover, was enhanced by his personal influence. For almost three decades Turgenev, who spent more time abroad than at home, was recognized as the ambassador of Russian letters in Europe. Friend of most outstanding representatives of European art and thought, he was a familiar figure in Western capitals, and the honorary degree awarded to him by the University of Oxford was but a small part of the homage paid to him by his devotees.

Yet despite his unique position and his wide following in almost every land, Turgenev's fortunes declined sharply in the twentieth century, when many reservations were formulated about his work and person. Some of these qualifications revived old discussions and repeated arguments known already in Turgenev's lifetime; some of them, however, were of more recent origin and expressed doubts peculiar to our century.

It is well known that most of Turgenev's illustrious French colleagues as well as Henry James and the Scandinavian-American Boyesen, who met the Russian personally, always spoke of him as being "completely Russian." The brothers Goncourt describe him in their *Journal* of 1863 as a "white haired giant who looked like the spirit of a mountain or a forest," an embodiment of Russian soil; Henry James stressed his eminently Russian characteristics and his preoccupation with Russian affairs; and after his death Renan said that "he was the incarnation of the whole race ... his conscience was in some sort the conscience of a people." It is curious that the main reservation of later times dealt precisely with the problem of Turgenev's national authenticity. There is still a widespread opinion that the author of *Fathers and Sons* became dear to readers outside Russia because of his European formation and his Western leanings. Alfred Kazin stated not long ago that Turgenev "seemed of all the great Russians the least characteristic"; the American critic understands perfectly why Henry James "found it so easy in 1878 to include an appreciation of Turgenev in *French Poets and Novelists.*" The familiar thesis is that Europeans and Americans of the last century loved Turgenev for his moderation, his conformity to the rules of Victorian art, and his lack of irritating and disturbing Russian national traits. The supporters of this opinion point out that Turgenev's novels and tales are as tame and respectable as their British counterparts of the same period; his heroines are not very different from the misses in the English family novels, and his nests of gentlefolk could be easily located in the countryside on the other side of the channel or even in Massachusetts or Rhode Island. Turgenev's urbane and restrained manners and his polished style, his gloss and grace, are considered as having been more suitable to and therefore more naturally appreciated in London and Boston than in Moscow and St Petersburg (not to speak of Leningrad).

When Tolstoy and Dostoevsky became known and widely read at the end of the nineteenth century and in the first decades of the twentieth century, they not only overshadowed Turgenev but were opposed to him as genuine interpreters of the Russian national scene. Compared to those two giants who shattered the world by the depth and frenzy of their moral and religious search, Turgenev lost in stature. Some critics advanced the theory that he was but an isolated phenomenon in Russian letters; that in any case he did not represent its main stream. His art, they argued, was strangely devoid of any serious moral intent, he never affirmed anything in any area of human endeavour, he never defended any doctrine and never fought on the side of any group. In this he differed fundamentally from other Russians. They were believers or searchers for truth and seekers after God, and he was an agnostic and a skeptic. He belonged much more to the old world of Western decadent culture than to the rising lands of the revolutionary East. And this is why, to quote Mr Kazin again, Turgenev's "civilized and European art seems no longer in the foreground of Russian literature but behind it." His unhappy noblemen and his delicately portrayed girls appeared elusive, sentimental, and pallid next to Dostoevsky's holy sinners and Tolstoy's robust, full blooded men and women. While the rest of Russian literature conveyed the feeling of exuberant vitality and deep passions, Turgenev's watercolors exuded melancholy and passivity, and his protagonists (except for Bazarov) talked and acted like second rate Werthers or poor versions of Hamlet. Was he not, in fact, the author of a story entitled *Hamlet of the Shchigrov District?*

One of the few Russians who did not try to preach and to win over the reader to some credo or idea, Turgenev became suspect even as a chronicler of his society. Russian critics had always interpreted Turgenev's novels as illustrations of the evolutionary process within the native educated classes between 1850 and 1880. Rudin (1855) represented the idealist of the forties, Lavretzky (1858) was typical of the fifties, *On the Eve* (1860) conveyed the atmosphere of expectation before the era of great reforms, and Bazarov in *Fathers and Sons* (1861) personified the new generation of nihilists. Later *Smoke* (1867) and *Virgin Soil* (1877) reflected the political debate and the beginnings of the populist movement. Already during Turgenev's lifetime his pictures of Russia started numerous discussions, and, as Edward Garnett said in his essay in 1917, provoked much angry heat and raised great clouds of acrimonious smoke because the defenders and the detractors of the writer disagreed about the historical accuracy of his representation. And fifty years after his death his importance as a social realist was questioned again. His portrayals of superfluous men afflicted by idleness or paralysis of the will seemed particularly inappropriate at a time when the Revolution had unleashed such an astounding amount of energy in Russia and transformed the whole country into an immense workshop. Not only was Turgenev lacking in "publicity value" but when things Russian were popular or when everybody was trying to solve the riddles of Russia's present regime, Turgenev could hardly help. Charles Morgan said in this connection that Turgenev was too unspectacular, too moderate and patient in spirit. Besides, his protagonists did not look like ancestors of twentieth-century Russians (again excepting Bazarov). And this led to an obvious conclusion: his novels and tales belonged to another age, they were visions of the past, and theirs was the quaint charm of early daguerrotypes in period frames. Turgenev was old fashioned, dated, and offered only an historical interest. Of course, it would be erroneous to identify any work of fiction with a straight representation of reality, but in Turgenev's case it was assumed that, while not making an exception to the rule, he was especially insensitive to Russia's historical development. He could not foresee its future and never went beyond the limitations of the small social group to which he belonged and which he depicted with an almost annoying monotony.

Doubts were also cast on Turgenev's art. In the nineteenth century even those who wondered about Turgenev's national authenticity or his social philosophy and historical accuracy recognized his craft and mastery. Yet the same George Moore who spoke of Turgenev's "unfailing artistry" in the eighties, later reproached him as having "a thinness, an irritating reserve," and repeated the quip of a British journalist who remarked that the Russian was "a very big man playing a very small instrument." The same George Moore echoed the discontent of the younger generation with Turgenev's lack of psychological depth: "he has often seemed to us to have left much unsaid, to have, as it were, only drawn the skin from his subject. Magnificently well is the task performed; but we should like to have seen the carcass disembowelled and hung up." Maurice Baring wrote in the twenties that Turgenev's works were dated, that he was inaccurate as a social historian and did not reflect the true Russia, and that his subject matter was too narrow. Others added in the thirties that Turgenev, this minor Hamlet who depicted unhappy love affairs of aristocratic ladies, covered only a small area of Russian reality. He was not sufficiently dynamic or varied, there was something effeminate about his manner, and his lyrical qualities were superficial. In general his art was too contrived and self conscious, its gentility simply expressing an organic lack of directness and vitality. A German critic of the thirties found "sweet and pleasant this art for convalescents which makes one agreeably drowsy."

While Marxist critics were inclined to see in Turgenev a "literary ghost from a sunken world of landed gentry" whose pessimism expressed the doom of his own class, others attacked the very smoothness of Turgenev's style. Alexis Remizov, an outstanding emigré novelist who appreciated Turgenev and refused to "simplify" problems deriving from his work, identified him nevertheless with the "Karamzine line of Russian letters": in the opinion of Remizov and many of his followers, Karamzine initiated in the eighteenth century that artificial literary idiom of the upper classes which abandoned the racy genuine language of the people and imitated the literary models of the West. The Karamzine-Turgenev-Chekhov trend of elegance, restraint, and linguistic refinement was opposed by the truly national tradition of pre-Petrine Russia with its down-to-earth realism, Greek-Orthodox and pagan roots, and popular vernacular. From that point of view Turgenev again was declared "unfit for our times, not representative as a Russian writer," edulcorated and conventional as an artist.

While all these criticisms were widespread in literary circles of the thirties, World War II and its aftermath brought about a change of heart and a revision of current judgments of Turgenev. Apparently readers both in Russia and the Western countries as well as throughout Asia (particularly in China and Japan) showed more stability than the critics: they did not seem to find Turgenev so dated as to drop him. Turgenev emerged as one of the most popular authors in the Soviet Union, particularly in the decade following the war with Hitler. Between 1948 and 1958 the USSR press turned out an average of three to four million copies of his works yearly, and in America and Europe there was a definite revival of interest. His novels and short stories were issued in new translations and found a large following among young and old.

It is evident that only few went to Turgenev for wisdom on the fate of communism or to gain some "first hand knowledge of Russia," a fashionable slogan of the time. But historians of literature and students of Turgenev suddenly discovered more profound reasons for his hundred-year hold over the general public. Charles Morgan, in an essay in his *Reflections in a Mirror* (1944), observed that Turgenev was criticised for his calm and his outward lack of dynamism, but then appropriately quoted Tolstoy's letter to Strakhov (Dostoevsky's biographer and disciple) after Turgenev's death: "The longer I live," wrote Tolstoy, "the more I like horses that are not restive. You say that you are reconciled to Turgenev. And I have come to love him very much, and curiously enough, just because he is not restive but gets to his destination. Turgenev will outlive Dostoevsky and not for his artistic qualities but because he is not restive."

Tolstoy pointed out that Turgenev's quiet tone was the result of control and not indifference. The strength of his understatement, enhanced by the neatness of his composition, was based on his essential humanity. Therefore it is erroneous to rank Turgenev with the representatives of the "well-made novel." Of course, he used the "dramatic technique," followed strictly the rule of the withdrawal of the author from his narrative, and built the latter on the revelation of characters through their actions and words. But he never tried to conceal his aversions and sympathies. The spontaneity of his emotional response and the freedom of his treatment of topics and characters made his works totally different from conventional Anglo-Saxon standards and from the French logical formality in constructing the "well-made novel."

What led to errors of evaluation were his serene diction and his belief that a good work of art must never lose its equilibrium or poise, even when dealing with anxiety and madness. He praised highly the "tranquillity in passion" of the French tragedian Rachel and spoke of her acting as a model of high esthetic fulfillment. Actually, the subject matter of Turgenev's novels and tales is far from idyllic: his love stories inevitably terminate in doom and frustration, and none of his novels has a happy ending, death striking most of his heroes. Throughout his works Turgenev displays an acute sense of the tragic in life and a constant preoccupation with man's condition on earth. Yet this pessimism is far from strident, and the writer's most poignant emotions and reflections are always expressed in an even voice, without outbursts of despair. Turgenev loves order, symmetry, balance, and radiance, and he presents a harmonized picture of life which makes his work appear self-contained. There is a world which can rightly be called "Turgenevian," and it stands in its own right as a complete and rounded achievement.

It could be argued that such an esthetic phenomenon is of sufficient importance to justify Turgenev's appeal in 1961. But other factors should be noted to understand the recent revival of interest in his work. Today we find Turgenev much more "authentically Russian" than did readers of half a century ago. *Fathers and Sons* should be required reading for anyone who wishes to understand the psychology of the Russian post-revolutionary generation. Bazarov is the forerunner of all the men of action in Soviet literature, in much the same way that Elena, Marianna, and Natalia are typical representatives of Russia's modern women. It is not difficult to discover that Turgenev's characters, despite their old fashioned garb, are more fundamentally national than many exotic figures of post-Turgenev fiction who were branded by sensation-craving readers as "true Russians."

For another thing, Turgenev, with his method of understatement (which Chekhov followed), is closer to modern literary trends than other realists of his own age. One can easily foresee that his tales — and they are probably the best and most enduring part of his work — will attract the attention and admiration of readers and writers for a long time, because they form a counterpart to the era of exaggerated psychologism which is rapidly approaching its decline. Nobody today will accuse Turgenev of "lack of psychological depth" or of over-simplicity. In his own unobtrusive manner, Turgenev hinted at all the complexities of the human soul and alluded to the hidden roots of human actions. In the dreams in Turgenev's works is an unsuspected wealth of psychological insight.

Virginia Woolf, in her last essays, wrote that "his books were curiously of our own time, undecayed, and complete in themselves. . . . His novels are so short and yet they hold so much. The emotion is so intense and yet so calm. The form is in one sense so perfect, in another so broken. They are about Russia in the fifties and sixties of the last century, and yet they are about ourselves at the present moment." What struck her as his greatest accomplishment was the union of fact and vision that he aimed at in all his writings. Turgenev himself formulated his ideal in a letter in which he said that the artist should not be simply satisfied to catch life in all its manifestations; he ought to understand them, to comprehend the laws according to which they evolve — even though those laws are not always visible.

While Turgenev's national authenticity has been fully reestablished in the last decade and his universality and perfection often stressed by Western and Russian writers, a revision has also taken place with regard to his "objectivity." The legend of his "impersonality" has been easily denounced by the psychological brand of criticism which found that Turgenev, as an individual, was prey to morbid complexes and obsessions, and suffered from many inner contradictions and fears. Already at the end of the nineteenth century George Moore assumed that "what influenced Turgenev's life is put forward in his books," and went on to argue that Turgenev exposed his own weaknesses and failures through the medium of his heroes and their unlucky experiences with life and women. Extremely representative of this trend in contemporary interpretation is the brilliant essay (1958) by Edmund Wilson which examines Turgenev's art in the light of his biography.

Of course the flow of literary fortune is in constant ebb, and the rejection of yesterday's formulae by critics and readers of our time is not final. Yet one has the feeling that we have overcome the biased and inimical judgments of the beginning of the century and particularly those of the twenties and thirties. Turgenev is returning to the Pantheon of world literature, not by sufferance but by merit. His lasting qualities as a story teller, as a painter of Russian life and character, and as an incomparable analyst of love seem more evident to us today than they did to the pre-war generation. He will remain a beloved writer for years to come — as long as elegiac grief combined with his exaltation of love and beauty and his vision of art as an orderly arrangement of emotional values can still quicken the feelings and the esthetic sense of men and women throughout the world.

M. S.

Sarah Lawrence College

Works by Turgenev

COLLECTED WORKS

COLLECTED EDITIONS

[Turgenieff's *Works*] New York, Holt etc 1867–85.   **1**

This series, although published not as a collected edition but as part of Holt's Leisure Hour series, often has binder's title, "Turgenieff's Works."

[1] *Fathers and sons*. Tr E. Schuyler. New York, Leypoldt & Holt 1867. 248 p

Reprinted 1872 by Holt. Also published with Lovell imprint [c1867]

[2] *Liza, or, A nest of nobles*. Tr W. R. S. Ralston. New York, Holt 1872. 318 p

Reprinted 1873.

[3] *Smoke*. Tr from the author's French version by William F. West. New York, Holt & Williams 1872. 291 p

Also published 1872 with Lovell imprint. Reprinted 1873.

[4] *Dimitri Roudine*. Tr from the French and German versions. New York, Holt & Williams 1873. 271 p

Reprinted from *Every Saturday* (see item 133).

[5] *On the eve*. Tr C. E. Turner. New York, Holt-Williams 1873. 272 p

Reprinted 1875.

[6] *Spring floods*. Tr Mrs Sophie Michell Butts. *A Lear of the steppe*. Tr from the French by William Hand Browne. New York, Holt 1874. 219 p

Also published 1874 with Lovell imprint.

[7] *Virgin soil*. Tr with the author's sanction by T. S. Perry. New York, Holt 1877. 315 p

This edition and the French version both appeared before the Russian edition which was published in 1878.

[8] *Annals of a sportsman*. Tr F. Abbott. New York, Holt 1885. 311 p

Turgenev protested against this translation which he felt to be inadequate.

[*The works of Ivan Turgénieff*] London, New York, Ward, Lock 1889. New ed. 5 v.   **2**

Contents:
Dimitri Roudine
Fathers and sons
Liza, or A noble nest. 318 p
Smoke
Virgin soil

This collection is cited in *The American Catalogue 1884–1890*, but the compilers have been unable to locate the set. The scant publishing evidence available leads us to deduce that Ward, Lock obtained the rights for these volumes from Holt and issued them both separately and in this collection, printing from the same plates.

Separate publication was as follows. *Dimitri Roudine* (1883); *Fathers and sons* (1883); *Smoke* (1883); *Virgin soil* (1883); and *Liza* (1884). (See *The English Catalogue of Books* iv 1881–1889.) These were presumably London imprints.

The novels of Ivan Turgenev. Tr Constance Garnett. Intro to vol 1–2 by S. Stepniak [pseud]; to vols 3–7, 12, 14–15 by Edward Garnett. London, Heinemann; New York, Macmillan 1894–99. 15 v. illus   **3**

v. 1. *Rudín*. 1894. 260 p
v. 2. *A house of gentlefolk*. 1894. 311 p
v. 3. *On the eve*. 1895. 290 p
v. 4. *Fathers and sons*. 1895. 359 p
v. 5. *Smoke*. 1896. 315 p
v. 6–7. *Virgin soil*. 1896. 244, 262 p
v. 8–9. *A sportsman's sketches*. 1895. 292, 284 p

Contents: Vol 8: Hor and Kalinitch. — Yermolai and the miller's wife. — Raspberry spring. — The district doctor. — My neighbour Radilov. — The peasant proprietor Ovsyanikov. — Lgov. — Byezhin prairie. — Kassyan of Fair Springs. — The agent. — The counting-house. — Biryuk. — Two country gentlemen. — Lebedyan.

Vol 9: Tatyana Borissovna and her nephew. — Death. — The singers. — Piotr Petrovitch Karataev. — The tryst. — The Hamlet of the Shtchigri district. — Tchertop-Hanov and Nedopyuskin. — The end of Tchertop-Hanov. — A living relic. — The rattling of wheels. — Epilogue: The forest and the steppe.

v. 10. *Dream tales and prose poems*. 1897. 324 p

Includes Clara Militch, Phantoms, The song of triumphant love, The dream. Poems in prose: The country, A conversation, The old woman, The dog, My adversary, The beggar, "Thou shalt hear the fool's judgment . . . ," A contented man, A rule of life, The end of the world, Masha, The fool, An eastern legend, Two stanzas, The sparrow, The skulls, The workman and the man with white

[17]

The novels of Ivan Turgenev, continued

hands, The rose, To the memory of U. P. Vrevsky, The last meeting, A visit, *Necessitas — vis — libertas!* Alms, The insect, Cabbage-soul, The realm of azure, Two rich men, The old man, The reporter, The two brothers, The egoist, The banquet of the supreme being, The sphinx, The nymphs, Friend and enemy, Christ, The stone, The doves, Tomorrow! Tomorrow! Nature, Hang him! What shall I think? "How fair, how fresh were the roses...," On the sea, N. N., Stay! Prayer, The Russian tongue.

v. 11. *The torrents of spring, and other stories.* 1897. 406 p

Includes First love, and Mumu.

v. 12. *A Lear of the Steppes, and other stories.* 1898. 318 p

Includes Faust, and Acia.

v. 13. *The diary of a superfluous man, and other stories.* 1899. 326 p

Includes A tour in the forest, Yakov Pasinkov, Andrei Kolosov, A correspondence.

v. 14. *A desperate character, and other stories.* 1899. 318 p

Includes A strange story, Punin and Baburin, Old portraits, The brigadier, Pyetushkov.

v. 15. *The Jew, and other stories.* 1899. 322 p

Includes An unhappy girl, The duellist, Three portraits, Enough.

Reprints:
—— London, Heinemann; New York, Macmillan 1906. 15 v.
—— London, Heinemann; New York, Macmillan 1916. 15 v.

Separate reprintings:

v. 1. *Rudín.* Reprinted 1912, 1917, 1919, 1920, 1921, 1930.

v. 2. *A house of gentlefolk.* Reprinted 1900, 1911, 1913, 1914, 1915, 1917, 1920. Another edition published 1921, 330 p; reprinted 1922, 1930.

v. 3. *On the eve.* Reprinted 1920, 1921, 1928.

v. 4. *Fathers and children.* Reprinted 1899, 1901, 1905, 1912, 1915, 1917, 1920, 1924, 1926 (1928 and 1932 in the series, The travellers library).

American edition published as *Fathers and sons.*

v. 5. *Smoke.* Reprinted 1901, 1904, 1912, 1915, 1917. New edition 1920, 330 p; reprinted 1921, 1928.

v. 6–7. *Virgin soil.* Reprinted 1901, 1913, 1915, 1917, 1920, 1921.

v. 8–9. *A sportsman's notebook.* Reprinted 1902, 1913, 1920, 1924.

v. 10. *Dream tales and prose poems.* Reprinted 1904, 1913, 1917, 1920, 1921.

v. 11. *The torrents of spring, and other stories.* Reprinted 1905, 1914, 1917, 1920, 1921.

v. 12. *A Lear of the steppes, and other stories.* Reprinted 1912, 1914, 1917, 1920.

v. 13. *The diary of a superfluous man, and other stories.* Reprinted 1920, 1921.

v. 14. *A desperate character, and other stories.* Reprinted 1911, 1917, 1920. New edition published 1921, 333 p.

v. 15. *The Jew, and other stories.* Reprinted 1913, 1919, 1920. Another edition published 1921, 337 p.

To this collection Heinemann added volumes 16 and 17 in 1921:

v. 16. *The two friends, and other stories.* 1921. 369 p

Includes Father Alexey's story, Three meetings, A quiet backwater.
Reprinted 1922.

v. 17. *Knock, knock, knock, and other stories.* 1921. 345 p

Includes The inn, Lieutenant Yergunov's story, The dog, The watch.
Reprinted 1922.

The complete set of 17 volumes was published by Heinemann and Macmillan in 1920–21.

The novels and stories of Iván Turgénieff. Tr Isabel Hapgood, with intro by Henry James. New York, Scribner 1903–04. 16 v. illus 4

v. 1–2. *Memoirs of a sportsman.* 1903. 308, 347 p

Contents: Vol 1: Khor and Kalinitch. — Ermolai and the miller's wife. — The raspberry water. — The district doctor. — My neighbour Radiloff. — Freeholder Ovsyanikoff. — Lgoff. — Byezhin meadow. — Kasyan from the Fair-Metcha. — The agent. — The counting-house. — The wolf. — Two landed proprietors.

Vol 2: Lebedyan. — Tatyana Borisovna and her nephew. — Death. — The singers. — Piotr Petrovitch Karataeff. — The tryst. — Hamlet of Shshtchigry county. — Tchertopkhanoff and Nedopiuskin. — The end of Tchertopkhanoff. — Living holy relics. — The rattling. — Epilogue: Forest and steppe.

v. 3. *Rudín: a romance. A King Lear of the steppes, and other stories.* 1903. 377 p

v. 4. *A nobleman's nest.* 1903. 307 p
v. 5. *On the eve.* 1903. 277 p
v. 6. *Fathers and children.* 1903. 352 p
v. 7. *Smoke.* 1904. 310 p
v. 8–9. *Virgin soil.* 1904. 273, 228 p
v. 10. *The Jew, and other stories.* 1904. 357 p

Includes Andréi Kólosoff, The bully, Pyetushkóff, The two friends.

v. 11. *The diary of a superfluous man, and other stories.* 1904. 344 p

Includes Three portraits, Three meetings, Mumu, The inn.

v. 12. *First love, and other stories.* 1904. 344 p.

Includes A correspondence, The region of dead calm, It is enough, The dog.

v. 13. *Phantoms, and other stories.* 1904. 321 p

Includes Yakoff Pasynkoff, Faust, An excursion to the forest belt, Asya.

v. 14. *The brigadier, and other stories.* 1904. 381 p

Includes The story of Lieutenant Ergunoff, A hapless girl, A strange story, Punin and Baburin.

v. 15. *Spring freshets, and other stories.* 1904. 372 p

Includes Knock, knock, knock; The watch.

v. 16. *A reckless character, and other stories.* 1904. 385 p

Includes The dream, Father Alexyei's story, Old portraits, The song of love triumphant, Clara Militch. Poems in prose: The village, A conversation, The old woman, The dog, The rival, The beggar man, "Thou shalt hear the judgment of the dullard . . . ," The contented man, The rule of life, The end of the world, Masha, The fool, An oriental legend, Two four-line stanzas, The sparrow, The skulls, The toiler and the lazy man, The rose, In memory of J. P. Vrévsky, The last meeting. The visit, Necessitas — vis — libertas, Alms, The insect, Cabbage-soup, The azure realm, Two rich men, The old man, The correspondent, Two brothers, The egoist, The supreme being's feast, The sphinx, Nymphs, Enemy and friend, Christ, The stone, Doves, To-morrow ! To-morrow ! Nature, "Hang him !" What shall I think? "How fair, how fresh were the roses," A sea voyage, N. N. Stay ! The monk, We shall still fight on ! Prayer, The Russian language.

Reprints:

—— London, Dent 1905. 16 v.
—— New York, Scribner 1906. 16 v.
—— New York, Scribner 1907. 16 v.
—— New York, Scribner 1922. 16 v.

Separate reprintings:

v. 1–2. *Memoirs of a sportsman.* Reprinted 1913, 1915, 1920, 1927.

v. 3. *Rudín . . . , and other stories.* Reprinted 1911, 1923.

v. 4. *A nobleman's nest.* Reprinted 1918, 1923, 1924.

v. 5. *On the eve.* Reprinted 1918, 1923.

v. 6. *Fathers and children.* Reprinted 1911, 1913, 1915, 1921, 1923, 1927, 1932.

v. 7. *Smoke.* Reprinted 1912, 1914, 1919, 1925.

v. 8–9. *Virgin soil.* Reprinted 1912, 1917, 1923, 1930.

v. 10. *The Jew, and other stories.* No reprints located.

v. 11. *The diary of a superfluous man, and other stories.* Reprinted 1915, 1923.

v. 12. *First love, and other stories.* Reprinted 1915, 1916, 1945.

v. 13. *Phantoms, and other stories.* Reprinted 1916, 1926.

v. 14. *The brigadier and other stories.* Reprinted 1916, 1923.

v. 15. *Spring freshets, and other stories.* Reprinted 1916, 1920, 1923, 1926.

v. 16. *A reckless character, and other stories.* Reprinted 1916, 1923.

The works of Iván Turgénieff. Tr Isabel Hapgood. Boston, Lauriat 1903–04. 14 v. in 7   5

v. 1. *Memoirs of a sportsman.* 308, 347 p; *A nobleman's nest.* 307 p (*Memoirs of a sportsman* has same contents as item 4, vols 1 and 2.)

v. 2. *Virgin soil.* 273, 228 p; [*A reckless character, and other stories,* including The dream, Father Alexyei's story, Old portraits, The song of triumphant love, Clara Militch, and Poems in prose] 385 p (Poems in prose has same contents as item 4, vol 16.)

v. 3. *Spring freshets, and other stories.* 372 p; *Smoke.* 310 p

Part 1 includes Knock, knock, knock; and The watch.

v. 4. *Rudín. A King Lear of the steppes.* 377 p; Phantoms, Yakoff Pasynkoff, Faust, An excursion to the forest belt, Asya. 321 p

v. 5. *The brigadier and other stories.* 381 p; *On the eve.* 277 p

Part 1 includes The story of Lieutenant Ergunoff, A hapless girl, A strange story, Punin and Baburin.

The works of Iván Turgénieff, continued

v. 6. *The diary of a superfluous man, and other stories.* 344 p; *Fathers and children.* 352 p

Part 1 includes Three portraits, Three meetings, Mumu, The inn.

v. 7. *First love and other stories.* 355 p; *The Jew and other stories.* 357 p

Part 1 includes A correspondence, The region of dead calm, It is enough, The dog. Part 2 includes Andrei Kolosoff, The bully, Pyetushkoff, The two friends.

This is substantially the Scribner edition, with only title-pages, and the order of volumes changed. The same plates were used. Another edition of 14 volumes in 7, also using the Scribner plates, was issued at the same time by the Jefferson Press, Boston, as a deluxe edition.

Other publishers of this same Lauriat set were Brentano, New York, who also reprinted the 14 v. in 7 in 1915 and 1916; and Himebaugh-Browne, New York, who apparently issued only a few of the 7 volumes. Scribner's again issued the 7 volumes in 1915, with the volume numbers altered. Lauriat reprinted the 7 volumes in 1914.

[*Works*] Tr I. [i. e. Rachelle S.] Townsend. **6**

Cited in Hershkowitz bibliography (see item 502) but unlocated. Miss Townsend translated several Russian novels for the Everyman series, including *Virgin soil* (see item 113).

The best known works of Ivan Turgenev, including Fathers and sons, Smoke, and five short stories. New York, Literary classics 193–? 375 p **7**

Includes A desperate character, A strange story, Punin and Baburin, Old portraits, The brigadier.

The best known works of Ivan Turgenev; including Fathers and sons; Smoke; and nine short stories. New York, Book League of America 1941. 502 p (Blue Ribbon books) **8**

This collection adds four stories to those published in item 7. The four stories are Pyetushkov, The Jew, An unhappy girl, and Three portraits.

The same collection was also published by Halcyon House (New York 1942) and by Doubleday (Garden City 1950).

Collected works of Ivan Turgenev, including Fathers and sons; Smoke; and nine short stories. New York, Greystone Press 195–? 502 p (Masterworks library) **9**

Includes A desperate character, A strange story, Punin and Baburin, Old portraits, The brigadier, Pyetushkov, The Jew, An unhappy girl, and Three portraits. This is same collection as item 8 with altered title.

Novels [Tr from the Russian by C. Garnett] London, Heinemann; New York, Macmillan 1951. 7 vols? **10**

Contents:
v. 1. Not published.
v. 2. *House of gentlefolk.* 181 p
v. 3. *On the eve.* 168 p
v. 4. *Fathers and children.* 214 p
v. 5. *Smoke.* 186 p
v. 6–7. *Virgin soil.* 2 v. 146, 159

Both MH and NNC have cataloged volumes from this set as parts of a collected edition. However, they were issued separately and in some cases without indication of their place in the series.

SELECTED STORIES AND PLAYS

The Borzoi Turgenev. Tr H. Stevens. Foreword by Serge Koussevitzky, intro by Avrahm Yarmolinsky. New York, Knopf 1950. 801 p **11**

Includes Smoke, Fathers and sons, First love, On the eve, Rudin, A quiet spot, and The diary of a superfluous man.

Reprinted 1955. Published in 1960 as paperback under title *The Vintage Turgenev.* New York, Vintage Books 1960. 2 v. 412, 391 p

Review: Helen Muchnic, Russian review ix No 4 (Oct 1950) 338–339

The district doctor, and other stories. Illus by Marvin Bileck. Emmaus, Pa, Story Classics 1951. 206 p illus **12**

Contents: The district doctor. — Yermolai and the miller's wife. — A strange story. — Foma, the wolf. — The counting-house. — A living relic. — A desperate character. — Pyetushkov. — [About the book, by E. J. Fluck.]

Fathers and children, and Rudin. Tr Richard Hare. London, Hutchinson International Authors 1947. 287 p **13**
Reprinted 1949.

First love; and, Púnin Babúrin. Tr by permission of the author, with biographical intro by Sidney Jerrold. London, Allen 1884. 237 p front **14**

First love. Tr I. Berlin. *Rudin, a romance.* Tr A. Brown, with intro by Lord David Cecil. New York, Pantheon Books; London, Hamilton 1950. 249 p **15**

A house of gentlefolk; and *Fathers and children*. Tr Constance Garnett. Ed William Allan Neilson, New York, Collier 1917. 406 p (Harvard classics) **16**

The Jew, and *Mumu*. New York, Little Leather Library 1918? 90 p **17**

Literary reminiscences and autobiographical fragments. Tr with intro by David Magarshack, and an essay on Turgenev by Edmund Wilson. New York, Farrar-Straus-Cudahy 1958. 309 p **18**

    Contents: Instead of an introduction. — A literary party at P. A. Pletnyov's. — Reminiscences of Belinsky. — Gogol, Zhukovsky, Krylov, Lermontov, Zagoskin. — A trip to Albano and Frascati. — Apropos of Fathers and sons. — The man in the grey spectacles. — My mates sent me! — The execution of Tropmann. — About nightingales. — Pégas. — Pergamos excavations. — The quail. — A fire at sea.

—— New York, Grove 1959. 309 p

—— London, Faber 1959. 272 p
    Reviews: Morris Philipson, *Commonweal* LXVIII (July 25, 1958) 428–430; Ernest J. Simmons, *Saturday Review* XLI (June 14, 1958) 22–23; Ewart Milne, *New Statesman* LVII No 1453 (Jan 17, 1959) 74–75

Moo-Moo; and The district doctor. Ed A. Raffi. London, Paul-Trench-Trubner 1917. 104 p **19**

—— New York, Dutton 1918.

Mumu, and The diary of a superfluous man. Tr Henry Gersoni. New York, Funk-Wagnalls 1884. 131 p (Standard library) **20**

Mumu; and Kassyan of Fair Springs. New York, Little Leather Library 191–? 94 p **21**

A nest of gentlefolk, and other stories. Tr with intro by Jessie Coulson. London, Oxford Univ Press 1959. 461 p (World's classics) **22**

    Includes A quiet backwater, First love, and A Lear of the steppes.

The plays of Ivan S. Turgenev. Tr M. S. Mandell. Intro by William Lyon Phelps. New York, Macmillan; London, Heinemann 1924. 583 p **23**

    Contents: Carelessness. Broke. Where it is thin, there it breaks. The family charge. The bachelor. An amicable settlement. A month in the country. The country woman. A conversation on the highway. An evening in Sorrento.

    Also published in two volumes, continuously paginated.

Selected tales. Tr with intro by David Magarshack. Garden City, N. Y., Doubleday 1960. xvii, 355 p (Anchor) **24**

    Includes The singers, Bezhin meadow, Mumu, Assya, First Love, Knock . . . knock . . . knock, Living relics, Clara Milich.

Three famous plays: A month in the country; A provincial lady; A poor gentleman. Tr Constance Garnett with intro by David Garnett. London, Duckworth; New York, Scribner 1951. 235 p illus **25**

—— New York, Hill Wang 1959. 235 p (Mermaid dramabook)

Three plays. Tr Constance Garnett. London, Cassell 1934. 323 p **26**

    Contents: A month in the country. A provincial lady. A poor gentleman.

Three short novels. Tr Constance Garnett. With appreciation of Turgenev by Henry James, Joseph Conrad, and Prosper Merimee. New York, Lear 1948. 352 p **27**

    Contents: First love. The diary of a superfluous man. Acia.

Three short novels: Asya, First love, Spring torrents. Tr I. and T. Litvinov. Moscow, Foreign Languages Publishing House 1955? 303 p **28**

An unfortunate woman, and Ass'ya. Tr Henry Gersoni. New York, Funk-Wagnalls 1886. 190 p (Standard library) **29**

SEPARATELY PUBLISHED WORKS

Annouchka; a tale. Tr from the French of the author's own translation, by Franklin Abbott. Boston, Cupples-Upham 1884. 111 p **30**

    Although Turgenev did oversee some translations of his work, he never himself translated any, as the above title-page seems to indicate.

The bachelor. A play in three acts, adapted by Miles Malleson. London, French 1953. 60 p illus **31**

"Bezhin meadows." From *A sportsman's sketches*. Tr C. Garnett. London, Heinemann; New York, Macmillan, n. d. **32**

"A daughter of Russia," Tr George W. Scott. New York, George Munro 1882. 17 p **33**

    The Seaside Library LX No 1216. "The *Seaside Library* was issued daily, and *A Daughter of Russia* appeared on March 7th. This series was published in the form of newsheets at 15 cents for an ordinary and 25 cents for a double number." *Bookman* LXXXIII (Dec 1932) p 201.

Don Quixote and Hamlet; a critical essay. Tr T. Rolleston. Dublin, Sealy-Bryers-Walker 190–? 30 p **34**

Fathers and children. Tr Richard Hare. Intro by Ernest J. Simmons. New York, Rinehart 1948. 233 p **35**

Fathers and sons. New York, Collier 1900? 348 p (The foreign classical romances) **36**

—— Tr Constance Garnett. Intro by Thomas Seltzer. New York, Boni-Liveright 1917. 243 p **37**

—— Intro by Carl Van Doren. New York, Literary Guild of America 192–? 242 p **38**

—— Tr C. Hogarth. London, Dent 1921. 276 p (Everyman) **39**
Reprinted 1929, 1934, 1938, 1941, 1954. New edition 1955 (item 52).

—— New York, Book League of America 1930. 243 p **40**

—— Tr Constance Garnett. New York, Grosset 1931. 242 p **41**

—— Intro by Carl Van Doren. New York, Literary Guild of America 1932. 242 p **42**

—— Tr Constance Garnett. Intro by Thomas Seltzer. New York, Modern Library 194–? 243 p **43**

—— Tr Constance Garnett, rev and ed by Lucy M. Cores. New York, Black 1942. 345 p (Classics club ed) **44**

—— Tr Constance Garnett, with foreword by Sinclair Lewis, illus with wood engravings by Fritz Eichenberg. New York, The Press of the Readers Club 1943. 234 p front, plates **45**

—— Tr B. Isaacs. Moscow, Foreign Languages Publishing House 1947. 206 p **46**

—— Tr Constance Garnett. Intro by Herbert J. Muller. New York, Modern Library 1950. 243 p **47**

—— Tr George Reavey. London, Hamilton; New York, Pantheon 1950. 247 p **48**

—— Illus by Konstantin Rudakov. Moscow, Foreign Languages Publishing House 1951. 213 p illus **49**

—— Tr Constance Garnett, with intro by Delmore Schwartz. New York, Harper 1951. 242 p **50**

—— Tr Constance Garnett, with preface by John T. Winterich and illus with wood engravings by Fritz Eichenberg. New York, Limited Editions Club 1951. 215 p illus **51**

—— Tr C. Hogarth. Intro by V. S. Pritchett. New York, Dutton 1955. 288 p **52**

—— A stressed text with intro and notes by E. R. Sands. London, Cambridge Univ Press 1955. 208 p **53**

—— Tr George Reavey. New York, Noonday Press 1958. 247 p (Noonday paperbacks) **54**
Reprint of 1950 edition.

—— New York, Collier 1958. 348 p **55**

—— Tr B. Makanowitzky. With intro by Alexandra Tolstoy. New York, Bantam Books 1959. 208 p **56**

—— Tr Constance Garnett. Illus by Fritz Eichenberg. New York, Heritage Press 1961. 234 p **57**

—— Tr Bernard Guilbert Guerney. With the author's comments on his book. New York, Modern Library 1961. 281 p **58**
Also published in college edition and in paperback.

First love. Moscow, Foreign Languages Publishing House 1953. 130 p **59**

—— Tr O. Gorchakov and illus by V. Sveshnikov. Moscow, Foreign Language Publishing House 1954. 137 p **60**

—— Tr Isaiah Berlin, with intro by Lord David Cecil. Illus by Fritz Wegner. London, Hamilton; Toronto, Collins 1956. 123 p **61**

Hamlet und Don Quixote, a critical essay. Tr with intro by M. Katz. n. p., Maisel & co 1910. 60 [4] p **62**
Cited in *National Union Catalog* (OCl), but not examined.

Hamlet and Don Quixote; an essay. Tr Robert Nichols. London, Hendersons 1930. 31 p **63**
Note on verso of title-page reads: "Of this edition 1000 copies have been printed, of which 105 copies are signed by the author." NjP has copy signed on title-page!

A house of gentlefolk. Tr F. M. Davis. London, Stodder & Houghton 1914? 1916? **64**
Not located. See *A nest of hereditary legislators* (item 77).

A hunter's sketches. Ed O. Gorchakov. Moscow, Foreign Language Publishing House 1955. 454 p **65**
Contents: Khor and Kalinich. — Yermolai and the miller's wife. — Raspberry spring. — The district doctor. — My neighbor Radilov. — The freeholder Ovsyanikov. — Lgov. — Bezhin mead. — Kasyan of fair springs. — The steward. — The countinghouse. — Biryuk. — Two country gentlemen. — Lebedyan. — Tatyana Borisovna and her nephew. — Death. — The singers.

WORKS BY TURGENEV

—— Pyotr Petrovich Karataev. — The tryst. — The Hamlet of the Shchigri district. — Chertopkhanov and Nedopyushkin. — The end of Chertopkhanov. — A living relic. The rattling of wheels. — The forest and the steppe.

[Letters] *Tourguéneff and his French circle.* Ed by E. Halperine-Kaminsky, tr from the French by E. Arnold. London, Unwin 1898. 302 p **66**

    Letters from Turgenev to Flaubert, Zola, and other friends in France.

Letters, a selection. Ed and tr by Edgar H. Lehrman. New York, Knopf 1961. 401 p illus, biblio **67**

    Reviews: David Magarshack, *New York Times Book Review* (Jan 22, 1961) p 6; Peter Melik, *National Review* x No 7 (Feb 25, 1961) 119–120.

Liza. Tr W. R. S. Ralston. London, Chapman-Hall 1869. 2 v. **68**

    Tr by Garnett as *A house of gentlefolk,* and by F. M. Davis as *A nest of hereditary legislators* (item 77).

—— Tr W. R. S. Ralston. London, Dent; New York, Dutton 1914. 231 p (Everyman) **69**

    Reprinted 1923, 1938, 1945.

A month in the country; a comedy in four acts. Tr M. Mandell, acting version by Rouben Mamoulian. New York, Rialto Service Bureau 1930. various paginations **70**

    Produced by the Theatre Guild at the Guild Theatre, New York, March 17, 1930.

—— Adapted into English by Emlyn Williams. London, Heinemann 1943. 93 p **71**

    Text based on literal trans by E. Fenn.

—— Adapted into English by Emlyn Williams with intro by Michael Belgrave. London, Heinemann 1953. 93 p **72**

—— Adapted into English by Emlyn Williams. New York, French 1957. 110 p **73**

Mumu. Tr Jessie Domb and Zlata Shoenberg. London, Harrap; New York, Transatlantic Arts 1945. 47, 47 p **74**

    Russian and English on opposite pages, numbered in duplicate.

—— Tr I. Litvinov. Moscow, Foreign Languages Publishing House 195–? 77 p illus **75**

A nest of the gentry. Tr Bernard Isaacs. Illus by Konstantin Rudakov. Moscow, Foreign Languages Publishing House 1947. 178 p illus **76**

    Reprinted 1951.

A nest of hereditary legislators. Tr F. M. Davis. London, Simkin & Marshall 1914. 396 p **77**

A nobleman's nest. Tr Richard Hare. London, Hutchinson International Authors 1949. 287 p **78**

On the eve. Tr C. E. Turner. London, Stodder & Houghton 1871. 248 p **79**

    Reprinted 1915, 1916.

—— Tr Richard Hare. London, Hutchinson International Authors 1947. 174 p **80**

—— Tr M. Budberg. New York, Chanticleer Press 1950. 225 p **81**

—— Tr M. Budberg. London, Cresset Press 1950. 217 p **82**

—— Tr G. Gardiner. Baltimore, Allen Lane 1950. 234 p (Penguin) **83**

—— Tr G. Gardiner. Harmondsworth, Middlesex, Penguin Books 1951. 233 p **84**

—— Tr S. Apresyan. Ed George H. Hanna. Moscow, Foreign Languages Publishing House 1959. 179 p **85**

Pegasus, Biryuk, Forest and steppe. Ed Nevill Forbes and E. G. Underwood. London, Oxford Univ Press 1917. 56 p **86**

    From *A sportsman's sketches.*

Poems in prose. Boston, Cupples-Upham 1883. 120 p port **87**

    Contents: The village. — The old woman. — A dialogue. — The dog. — My opponent. — An axiom. — Dost thou hearken to the words of the fool. — The beggar. — A contented man. — The destruction of the world. — Mascha. — The blockhead. — An oriental legend. — Two quatrains. — The sparrow. — The laborer and the man with the white hand. — The skull. — The last meeting. — The rose. — The visit. — Necessitas-vis-libertas. — The alms. — The insect. — The cabbage-soup. — The happy land. — Who is the richer? — The old man. — The newspaper correspondent. — Two brothers. — In memory of I. P. W. — The egotist. — The supreme being's banquet. — The nymphs. — The sphinx. — The friend and the enemy. — Christ. — The stone. — The doves. — To-morrow, to-morrow ! — Nature. — Hang him ! — What shall I think about? — How lovely and fresh those roses were ! — A trip by sea. — N. N. — Stop ! — The monk. — Let's keep a good heart. — Prayer. — The Russian language.

    Also appeared with New York, Putnam's c1883 imprint.

—— 2d ed. Boston, DeWolfe, Fiske 1883. 120 p **88**

    Reprinted 1887.

Poems in prose, continued

—— A metrical version by J. B. Mather. Adelaide, Advertiser Newspapers 1934. 98 p   **89**

Contents: In the village. — A dialogue. — The old woman. — The dog. — My adversary. — The beggar. — The fool's judgment thou wilt hear. — A contented man. — A rule of life. — The end of the world. — Masha. — A blockhead. — An eastern tale. — The two poets. — The sparrow. — The skulls. — The working man and the man with the white hands. — The rose. — In memoriam. — The last good-bye. — A visit. — Necessitas-vis-libertas. — The alms. — The insect. — Cabbage soup. — The fields of the blest. — Which is the richer? — The old man. — The reporter. — The two brothers.—The egoist. — Jupiter's feast. — The sphinx. — The nymphs. — Friend and foe. — Christ. — The stone. — The doves. — To-morrow! to-morrow! — Nature. — Hang him. — What shall I think? — How were the roses so fresh and so fair?. — On the sea. — N. N. — Abide. — The monk. — We are still at war. — Prayer. — The Russian language.

—— Tr Eugenia Schimanskaya. Drawings by Donia Nachshen. London, Drummond 1945. 66 p illus   **90**

Contents: The village. — The conversation. — The old woman. — The dog. — The rival. — The beggar. — "You shall hear the judgment of the fool." — The contented man. — Worldly wisdom. — The end of the world. — Masha. — An eastern tale. — Two quatrains. — The sparrow. — The skulls. — The worker and the man with white hands. — The rose. — The memory of U. P. Vrevskaya. — The last meeting. — The visit. — Necessitas-vis-libertas. — Charity. — The insect. — Cabbage soup. — The realm of azure. — Two rich men. — The old man. — The journalist. — Two brothers. — The egotist. — The feast of the supreme being. — The sphinx. — The nymphs. — Enemy and friend. — Christ. — The stone. — Two doves. — To-morrow! To-morrow! — Nature. — Hang him. — What shall I be thinking? — "How lovely, how fresh were the roses . . . " — A sea voyage. — N. N. — Stay! — The monk. — We'll still go on fighting! — Prayer. — The threshold. — The Russian language.

—— In Russian and English, ed André Mazon. Tr C. Garnett and R. Rees. Oxford, Blackwell 1951. 219 p (Blackwell's Russian texts)   **91**

Contents: The country. — The old woman. — A meeting. — The beggar. — My adversary. — I feel pity. — A conversation. — The dog. — Friend and enemy. — Thou shalt hear the fool's judgment. — A contented man. — A curse. — The twins. — The blackbird (I, II). — A bird without a nest. — The cup. — Whose fault? — The fool. — The workman and the man with white hands. — The banquet of the supreme being. — The skulls. — An eastern legend. — The end of the world. — Two stanzas. — The rose. — Masha. — Necessitas, vis, libertas. — The sparrow. — The last meeting. — A rule of life. — A visit. — The threshold. — The insect. — A snake. — Cabbage soup. — Author and critic. — On arguing. — The reporter. — The old man. — Oh, my youth. — To***. — Two rich men. — Two brothers. — To the memory of Yu. P. Vrevskaya. — I walked amid high mountains. — When I am no more. — Christ. — The hour glass. — The nymphs. — The egoist. — The sphinx. — Alms. — The stone. — The doves. — To-morrow! To-morrow! — I rose from my bed at night. — The realm of azure. — Nature. — Hang him!. — How fair, how fresh were the roses. — What shall I think? — When I am alone. — To N. N. — On the sea. — The monk. — Stay! — We will still fight on. — The path to love. — Phrases. — Simplicity. — The Brahmin. — You wept. — Love. — Prayer. — Truth and justice. — The partridges. — Nessun maggior dolore. — The Russian tongue. — On the rack. — A rule of life. — A baby's cry. — My trees.

"Notes" by Charles Salomon.

A provincial lady. A comedy in one act. A new version by Miles Malleson. London, French 1950. 44 p illus   **92**

Punin and Babwin. Tr George Scott. New York, Munro 1882. 18 p (Seaside Library)   **93**

The ruffian. Tr from the German. Chicago, Overland Library 1887. (Collection Schick, no 13)   **94**

Russian life in the interior; or The experiences of a sportsman. Ed James D. Meiklejohn. Edinburgh, Black 1855. 428 p   **95**

Translated from M. Charriere's French version of *A sportsman's notebook*, a version against which Turgenev strongly protested.

Contents: Khor and Kalinytch. — Ermolai and the miller's wife. — Raspberry water. — The country doctor. — My neighbour Radiloff. — The Odnovoretz. — Lgoff. — Beejina Lough. — The funeral. — The bourmister. — The counting house. — Foma the bireouk. — The two village lords. — Lebediana. — The provincial woman, and her nephew the artist. — How a Russian dies. — The tavern. — Karataeff. — The assignation. — The higher provincial society. — Native oddities. — The forest and the steppe — Epilogue.

Senilia. Poems in prose, being meditations, sketches. . . . English version with intro and biographical sketch by S. Macmullan. Bristol, Arrowsmith 1890. 153 p   **96**

Smoke, or Life at Baden, a novel. Tr from the French version. London, R. Bentley 1868. 2 v.   **97**

   Another bad translation (anonymous) against which Turgenev protested.

—— Intro by John Reed. New York, Modern Library 1919. 234 p   **98**

—— London, Heinemann 1930. 315 p (The traveller's library)   **99**

—— Tr Natalie Duddington. London, Dent 1949. 242 p; New York, Dutton 1950. 256 p (Everyman)   **100**

Song of triumphant love. Adapted by Marian Ford. New York, Munro 1882. 17 p (Seaside library 72)   **101**

A sportsman's notebook. Tr Charles and Natasha Hepburn. London, Cresset Press; New York, Chanticleer Press 1950. 397 p   **102**

   Contents: Khor and Kalinich. — Ermolai and the miller's wife. — Raspberry water. — The country doctor. — My neighbour Radilov. — Ovsyanikov the freeholder. — Lgov. — Bezhin meadow. — Kasyan from Fair Springs. — The bailiff. — The estate office. — The bear. — Two landowners. — Lebedyan. — Tatyana Borisovna and her nephew. — Death. — The singers. — Pyotr Petrovich Karataev. — The rendezvous. — Prince Hamlet of Shchigrovo. — Chertopkhanov and Nedopyuskin. — The end of Chertopkhanov. — The live relic. — The knocking. — Forest and steppe.

—— Tr Charles and Natasha Hepburn. New York, Viking Press 1956. 403 p   **103**

—— Tr Charles and Natasha Hepburn. New York, Viking Press; Toronto, Macmillan 1957. 397 p (Compass books)   **104**

   Items 103–104 have same contents as 102.

A sportsman's sketches. Tr Constance Garnett. New York, Dutton 1932. 253 p illus.   **105**

   This edition contains fourteen of the twenty-five sketches which appeared in the two volumes of the collected edition. Not located.

Spring floods. Tr E. Richter. London, Lamley 1895. 252 p   **106**

Tales from the note-book of a sportsman. Tr E. Richter. Series 1. London, Lamley 1895. 247 p   **107**

The torrents of spring. Tr David Magarshack. New York, Farrar, Straus and Cudahy; London, Hamilton 1959. 188 p   **108**

—— Tr David Magarshack. Toronto, Collins 1960. 188 p (Deluxe edition)   **109**

The two friends. Tr Noel Evans. London, Paul-Trench-Trubner 1936. 115 p   **110**

The unfortunate one; a novel. Tr A. R. Thompson. London, Trubner 1888. 134 p   **111**

Virgin soil. Tr A. Dilke. London, Macmillan 1878. 346 p   **112**

—— Tr Rachelle Townsend. Intro by Ernest Rhys. London, Dent 1911. 317 p (Everyman)   **113**

   Reprinted 1915, 1916, 1920, 1929, 1942, 1948, 1954. New edition published 1955, 336 p.

—— Tr Constance Garnett. New York, Grove Press 1956. 305 p (Evergreen)   **114**

ARTICLES, STORIES, AND POEMS PUBLISHED IN ANTHOLOGIES AND PERIODICALS

"The adventure of Second Lieutenant Bubnov," In *And the darkness falls* ed by Boris Karloff. Cleveland, World 1946. 58–65   **115**

"After death," *Modern age* ? (New York 1883)   **116**

   "Klara Milich."

"The antchar," *Galaxy* xv Nos 3, 4 (Mar–Apr 1873) 330–350, 461–480   **117**

   "A quiet backwater."

"Apropos of 'Fathers and Sons,'" *Partisan review* xxv No 2 (Spring 1958) 265–273   **118**

   See also item 18.

"Assja," *Galaxy* xxiii No 3 (Mar 1877) 368–394   **119**

"Asya," In *Selected Russian short stories* comp and tr Alfred E. Chamot. New York, Oxford Univ Press 1925. 107–160   **120**

"Autumn," *Arena* ii No 12 (Nov 1890) p 705   **121**

"Autumn," continued

—— Tr by Maud Jerrold. *Slavonic review* x No 28 (Jul 1931) p 24 **122**

"Ballad," In *The wagon of life* tr Cecil Kisch. New York, Oxford Univ Press 1947. p 42 **123**

"Beneficence and gratitude," In *The world's best humor* ed C. Wells. New York 1933. p 638 **124**

"The brigadier," Tr by Constance Garnett. *Outlook* LXXXVIII No 4 (Jan 25, 1908) 223–238 port **125**

    Intro by Hamilton W. Mabie, 223–226.

"The bully," Tr by Mary J. Safford. *Living Age* CCXI Nos 2732–36 (Nov 14, 21, 28; Dec 5, 12, 1896) 387–393, 483–490, 547–549, 636–642, 700–704 **126**

"Clara Militch; a tale," Tr by Augustus Anthony and Walter W. Spooner. *The independent* XXXVI Nos 1871–1873 (Oct 9, 16, 23, 1884) 1306–08, 1338–40, 1370–72 **127**

"A conversation," *Current literature* XLII No 4 (Apr 1907) p 465 **128**

"A correspondence," *Galaxy* XII No 4 (Oct 1871) 451–469 **129**

"The country," In *The world's best essays, from Confucius to Mencken* ed F. H. Pritchard. New York, Halcyon House 1939. 730–731 **130**

Item not used **131**

"Desperate," *Cosmopolitan* V No 4 (Aug 1888) 335–344 **132**

Dimitri Roudine. In *Every Saturday* III Nos 4–17 (Jan 25 – Apr 26, 1873) 85, 113, 141, 169, 197, 225, 253, 281, 309, 337, 365, 393, 421, 449 **133**

    See also item 1 [vol 4].

"The dream," Tr Isabel Hapgood. In *Great Russian short stories* ed Stephen Graham. New York, Liveright 1929. 169–192 **134**

    Reprinted London, Benn 1959.

"Dying plea to Tolstoy," In *A treasury of Russian life and humor* ed John Cournos. New York, Coward-McCann 1943. p 79 **135**

"Evening in the country," In *The Slav anthology* tr Edna Underwood. Portland, Me., Mosher Press 1931. 210–211 **136**

Fathers and sons. In *A treasury of Russian literature* ed Bernard Guilbert Guerney. New York, Vanguard Press 1943. 255–436 **137**

—— [excerpt] In *Anthology of Russian literature* ed Leo Wiener. New York, Putnam's 1903. 282–295 **138**

—— [excerpt] In *The world's greatest books* ed Alfred Harmsworth and S. S. McClure. [n. p.] McKinley, Stone & Mackenzie 1910. 245–259 **139**

"Faust," *Galaxy* XIII Nos 5, 6 (May–Jun 1872) 621–634, 734–746 **140**

—— *Fortnightly review* LXII Ns LVI No 3311 (Jul 1, 1894) 132–160 **141**

"A fire at sea," *Macmillan's magazine* LIV No 319 (May 1886) 39–44 **142**

—— *Eclectic magazine* Ns XLIII No 6 (Jun 1886) 835–839 **143**

—— *London magazine* IV no 7 (1957) 18–24 **144**

—— *Reporter* XVIII No 4 (Feb 20, 1958) 31–34 **145**

First love. Tr C. Garnett. In *Love throughout the ages* ed Robert Lynd. New York, Coward-McCann 1932. 685–734 **146**

—— *Golden book magazine* XVI Nos 94–96 (Oct–Dec 1932) 339–352, 420–433, 562–575 **147**

—— In *World's great love novels* ed Edwin Seaver. Cleveland, World 1944. **148**

—— In *Great Russian short novels* ed Philip Rahv. New York, Dial Press 1951. 39–109 **149**

—— Tr Constance Garnett and N. H. Dole. In *Four great Russian short novels*. New York, Dell 1959. 9–73 **150**

"Freddy," In *Russian songs and lyrics* . . . ed John Pollen. London, East and West 1917. 159–160 **151**

"Ghosts," In *Tales for a stormy night*. Tr from the French. Cincinnati, Clarke 1891. 3–67 **152**

"Hamlet and Don Quixote," Tr J. Kral and P. Durdik. *Poet lore* IV (1892) 169–183 **153**

—— *Fortnightly review* LXII Ns LVI No 332 (Aug 1, 1894) 191–205 **154**

—— [excerpt] In *A treasury of Russian life and humor* ed John Cournos. New York, Coward-McCann 1943. 26–30 **155**

"Hamlet and Don Quixote, the Two Eternal Human Types," *Current literature* XLII No 3 (Mar 1907) 290–293 **156**

"I wander round the lake," Tr by M. Jerrold. *Slavonic review* x No 29 (Dec 1931) p 272 **157**

"The idiot," Tr by W. R. S. Ralston. *Temple Bar* XXIX (May 1870) 249–266   **158**

"In front of the guillotine," In *Bachelor's quarters; stories from two worlds* ed Norman Lockridge. New York, Biltmore 1944. 689–709 **159**

"King Lear of the Russian steppes," Tr Bury Palliser. *London society* XXII No 131 (Nov 1872) 437–449   **160**

—— [excerpt] *Every Saturday* II No 22 (Nov 30, 1872) 608–613   **161**
Reprinted from *London society*, item 160.

—— *Living age* CXVI No 1491 (Jan 4, 1873) 48–57   **162**

"The kiss," Tr by Bernard Guerney. *Golden book magazine* XII No 69 (Sep 1930) p 79 **163**

"Krilof and his fables," [review of Ralston translation] *Academy* II (Jul 15, 1871) p 345
Written in English.   **164**

The lady from the provinces; a comedy in one act. Tr Jenny Covan. In *The Moscow art theatre series of Russian plays* ed O. M. Sayler. New York, Brentano 1923. vol 5, 45–90   **165**

"A Lear of the steppe," *Southern magazine* XI (Nov–Dec 1872) 513, 641   **166**

"A Lear of the steppes," Tr C. Garnett. In *The book of the short story* ed Alexander Jessup and H. S. Canby. New York, Appleton 1912. 359–438   **167**

—— Tr Constance Garnett. In *Russian short stories* ed Harry C. Schweikert. Chicago, Scott-Foresman 1919. 113–206   **168**

—— Tr Constance Garnett. In *Great short novels of the world* ed B. H. Clark. New York, McBride; London, Heinemann 1927.   **169**

—— Tr Constance Garnett. In *Representative modern short stories* ed Alexander Jessup. New York, Macmillan 1929. 226–303   **170**

—— Tr Constance Garnett. In *A treasury of great Russian short stories; Pushkin to Gorky* ed Avrahm Yarmolinsky. New York, Macmillan 1944. 143–214   **171**

LETTERS

"Tourguenieff's letters," Tr Florence K. Wischnewetsky. *Overland monthly* 2nd ser VIII No 46 (Oct 1886) 385–389   **172**

"Some new letters of Tourgeniev," Tr and ed Rosa Newmarch. *Atlantic monthly* LXXXIV No 505 (Nov 1899) 691–705.   **173**

"Turgeneff's German letters," intro by E. Halperine-Kaminsky. *Saturday review* CVII–CVIII Supplements for Feb 6, 13, 20, 27, Mar 6; Aug 7, 14, 21, 28, Sep 4, 1909   **174**

"Tolstoi and Turgenev: extracts from correspondence," *Living age* CCCXXIX No 4265 (Apr 4, 1926) 197–200   **175**

"Turgenev's last letter," [letter to Tolstoy unsigned, July 3, 1883] in *The Portable Russian reader* ed Bernard Guilbert Guerney. New York, Viking Press 1947. 627–628   **176**
Reprinted 1959.

"Lettres de Tourguéneff à Henry James," ed Jean Seznec. *Comparative literature* I No 3 (Summer 1949) 193–209   **177**
Some of the letters are in English.

* * *

"Makel-Adel," In *Mainly horses* ed Ernest Rhys and C. A. Dawson-Scott. New York, Appleton 1929. 265–280   **178**

—— In *A treasury of animal stories* ed Emma Louise Mally. New York, Citadel Press 1946. 202–214   **179**

"Monsieur François; a souvenir of 1848," *Fortnightly review* XCVI Ns XC No 539 (Nov 1, 1911) 946–961   **180**

A month in the country. Tr G. Noyes. In *Masterpieces of the Russian drama* ed G. Noyes. New York 1933. 233–327   **181**

A month in the country; a comedy in five acts. Tr M. Mandell. In *Famous plays of 1937*. London 1937. 9–159   **182**

A month in the country. Adapted into English by Emlyn Williams. In *Great Russian plays* ed Norris Houghton. New York, Dell 1960. 123–218 (Laurel drama series)   **183**

"Moomoo," Tr Constance Garnett. In *A treasury of great Russian short stories; Pushkin to Gorky*. New York, Macmillan 1944. 116–142   **184**

"Mou-Mou," *Lippincott's monthly magazine* VII (Apr 1871) 372–387   **185**

"Mumu," Tr C. Garnett. In *Stories by foreign authors; Russian*. New York 1898. 11–61 **186**

—— In *Writers of the Western world* ed Clarence A. Hibbard. Boston, Houghton-Mifflin 1942. 959–972   **187**

—— Tr C. Garnett. In *Representative short stories* ed Amanda M. Ellis. New York, Ronald Press 1946. 469–506   **188**

"Mumu," continued

—— In *Famous dog stories* ed Page Cooper. New York, Doubleday 1948. 1–19 **189**

A nest of nobles [excerpt] In *The world's greatest books* ed Alfred Harmsworth and S. S. McClure. [n. p.] McKinley, Stone & Mackenzie 1910. 259–272 **190**

"New poems in prose," Tr by George Z. Patrick and George R. Noyes. *Slavonic review* XII No 35 (Jan 1934) 241–257 **191**

"The nihilist" [excerpt from *Fathers and sons*] In *Half-hours with foreign novelists* (See item 348.)

"The nobleman of the steppe," Tr H. H. Boyesen. *Scribner's monthly* XIV No 3 (Jul 1877) 313–338 **192**

"Old portraits," Tr C. Garnett. In *A treasury of great Russian short stories; Pushkin to Gorky* ed Avrahm Yarmolinsky. New York, Macmillan 1944. 228–249 **193**

—— In *The heritage of European literature* ed Edward Howell Weatherly. Boston, Ginn 1948–49. vol 2, 506–517 **194**

"On the road," Tr by M. Jerrold. *Slavonic review* IX No 25 (Jun 1930) p 207 **195**

—— In *The wagon of life* tr C. Kisch. New York, Oxford Univ Press 1947. p 41 **196**

—— Tr by W. Matthews. *Slavonic review* XXVIII No 70 (Nov 1949) p 4 **197**

"One may spin a thread too finely; a comedy in one act," Tr Margaret Gough. *Fortnightly review* LXXXV Ns XCI No 508 (Apr 1, 1909) 786–804 **198**

"Pegasus," Tr by F. H. Snow and A. M. Nikolaieff. *Golden book magazine* VIII No 44 (Aug 1928) 243–246 **199**

POEMS IN PROSE

"The Blockhead," *Romance* XV No 1 (Jul 1894) 44–45 **200**

"Cabbage-soup," *Golden book magazine* IV No 19 (Jul 1926) p 2 **201**

—— In *The mother's anthology* ed William Lyon Phelps. New York, Doubleday 1940. p 352 **202**

"Dear Mary," In *Russian songs and lyrics* tr John Pollen. London, East and West 1917. 182–186 **202A**

"Masha."

"The dog," *Living age* CCXXI No 2866 (Jun 10, 1899) 776–785 **203**

—— In *Short stories*. New York 1900. vol 37, 220–234 **204**

—— *Fortnightly review* XC Ns LXXXIV (Aug 1, 1908) 341–352 **205**

—— In *Golden book of dog stories* ed Era Zistel. Chicago, Ziff-Davis 1947. 241–253 **206**

"The egotist," *Dublin review* XCV Ns XLIII (Jul 1884) 64 **207**

"The fool," *Century magazine* XXVII No 2 (Dec 1883) 319–320 **208**

"How beautiful were once the roses," In *The silver treasury* ed Jane Manner. New York, French 1934. 148–149 **209**

"Nature," In *Anthology of Russian literature* ed Leo Wiener. New York, Putnam 1902–03. vol 2, 295–296 **210**

"Nymphs," Tr by Isabel Hapgood. *Golden book magazine* III No 17 (May 1926) p 688 **211**

"Prayer," In *The world's best humor* ed C. Wells. New York 1933. p 638 **212**

"A rule of life," *Golden book magazine* XI No 61 (Jan 1930) p 92 **213**

"The Russian language," In *Russian songs and lyrics* tr John Pollen. London, East and West 1917. p 186 **214**

"The Russian tongue," In *A treasury of Russian life and humor* ed John Cournos. New York, Coward-McCann 1943. p 2 **215**

—— In *A treasury of Russian literature* ed Bernard Guilbert Guerney. New York, Vanguard Press 1943. p vii **216**

"The sparrow," In *Short stories*. New York 1895. vol 20, p 230 **217**

—— In *The world's best essays, from Confucius to Mencken* ed F. H. Pritchard. New York, Halcyon House 1939. 731–732 **218**

"The threshold," Tr Herman Bernstein. *Independent* LX No 2985 (Feb 15, 1906) p 386 **219**

—— *New republic* XXIX No 375 (Feb 28, 1922) p 309 **220**

—— In *The Russian horizon; an anthology* comp Nagendranath Ganguli. London, Allen-Unwin 1943. p 42 **221**

—— In *A treasury of Russian life and humor* ed John Cournos. New York, Coward-McCann 1943. 30–31 **222**

"Tomorrow! to-morrow!" *Dublin review* xcv Ns xliii (Jul 1884) 64–65 **223**

"Treasure," *All the year round* Ns x No 253 (Oct 4, 1873) 543–547 **224**
An abridged version of "The dog."

"Two stanzas: A barbed satire on literary success," *Golden book magazine* xix No 114 (Jun 1934) 703–704 **225**

"A visit," Tr J. H. Wisby. In *Short stories*. New York 1893. vol 12, p 445 **226**

* * *

"The priest's son," *Lippincott's magazine* xix (Jun 1877) 744–750 **227**

"A quiet backwater," In *Russian short stories*. London, Faber; Toronto, Ryerson 1943. 78–150 **228**

Review of *History of a Town* by M. E. Saltykoff (Shchedrin), *Academy* ii (Mar 1, 1871) 151–152 **229**
Written in English.

"A Russian sorcerer," *Appleton's journal* iii No 43 (Jan 22, 1870) 94–99 **230**

"Senilia; prose poems," *Macmillan's magazine* xliv Nos 289–290 (Nov–Dec 1883) 9–20, 103–116 **231**
Contents: Part I: In the village. — A conversation. — The old woman. — My dog. — The adversary. — The beggar. — "Accept the verdict of fools. . . . " — A self-satisfied man. — A rule of life. — The end of the world. — Mascha. — The blockhead. — An Eastern legend. — The two quatrains. — The sparrow. — The skulls.
Part II: The workman and the man with the white hands. — The rose. — Alms. — The insect. — The cabbage soup. — The happy land. — Who is the richer? — Old age. — The newspaper correspondent. — Two brothers. — To the memory of J. P. W-Skaja. — The egoist. — The banquet of the deity. — The sphinx. — The nymphs. — The enemy and the friend. — Christ. — The stone. — The doves. — Nature. — Hang him! — "The roses were lovely, the roses were fresh. . . . " — A sea voyage. — The monk. — We will struggle. — Prayer. — The Russian language.

"Serenade," In *Russian poems* ed Charles F. Coxwell. London, Daniel 1929. p 165 **232**

"Sketches and reminiscences," Tr C. Turner. *Macmillan's magazine* xliv No 262 (Aug 1881) 306–320 **233**

Reprinted in *Appleton's journal* xxvi (1881) 305–315; *Eclectic magazine* Ns xxxiv (1881) 440–452; *Living age* cl (1881) 692–703.

Smoke [excerpt] In *The world's greatest books* ed Alfred Harmsworth and S. S. McClure. [n. p.] McKinley, Stone & Mackenzie 1910. 272–286 **234**

"The song of love triumphant," Tr I. Hapgood. In *Great Russian short stories* ed Stephen Graham. New York, Liveright 1929. 144–169 **235**
Reprinted London, Benn 1959.

—— Tr by Constance Garnett. *Golden book magazine* xv No 85 (Jan 1932) 69–81 **236**

—— *Cosmopolitan* ii No 1 (Sep 1886) 3–14 **237**

—— In *Little masterpieces of fiction* ed Hamilton W. Mabie and L. Strachey. New York, Doubleday 1904. vol 1, 123–154 **238**

"Specters, a phantasy," In *The portable Russian reader* ed Bernard Guilbert Guerney. New York, Viking Press 1947. 103–141 **239**
Editor's note 100–103.

SKETCHES FROM
A SPORTSMAN'S NOTEBOOK

"Photographs from Russian life," *Fraser's magazine* l (Aug 1854) 209–222 **240**
Quotes long passages with some critical comment.

Four extracts published in *Household words*:
"The children of the czar" [The agent], *Household words* xi No 258 (Mar 3, 1855) 108–114 **241**

"More children of the czar" [Pietr Petrovich Karatoev], *Household words* xi No 263 (Apr 7, 1855) 227–232 **242**

"Nothing like Russian leather" [Lgov], *Household words* xi No 265 (Apr 21, 1855) 286–288 **243**

"A Russian singing match" [The singers], *Household words* xii No 296 (Nov 24, 1855) 402–405 **244**

"Bezhin meadow," In *Great Russian short stories* ed Stephen Graham. New York, Liveright 1929. 192–218 **245**
Reprinted London, Benn 1959.

—— In *Great Russian short stories* ed Norris Houghton. New York, Dell 1958. 63–84 **246**

"Biryuk," Tr Constance Garnett. In *Russian short stories* ed Harry C. Schweikert. Chicago, New York, Scott-Foresman 1919. 103–112 **247**

"Biryuk," continued

—— Tr Constance Garnett. In *Our heritage of world literature* ed Stith Thompson. New York, Dial Press 1938. 764–768 **248**
Reprinted New York, Dryden Press 1942.

—— Tr C. Garnett. In *Adventures in world literature* ed R. B. Inglis and W. K. Stewart. New York, Harcourt-Brace 1946. 785–793 **249**

"Byezhin meadow," In *The house of fiction; an anthology of the short story* ed Caroline Gordon and Allen Tate. New York, Scribner 1950. 129–145 **250**

"Byezhin prairie," from *A sportsman's sketches.* In *The Warner library.* New York, Knickerbocker Press 1917. vol 25, 15091–106 **251**

"The counting-house," Tr Constance Garnett. In *Short story classics* ed William Patten. New York, Collier 1907. vol 1, 81–106 **252**

—— *Famous story magazine* I No 3 (Dec 1925) 332–340 **253**

"The district doctor," In *Short story masterpieces* ed Joseph B. Esenwein. Springfield, Mass., The home correspondence school 1912. vol 3, 139–156 **254**

—— done into English by John Cournos. *Lippincott's monthly magazine* XLI No 542 (1913) 233–246 **255**

—— In *Best Russian short stories* ed Thomas Seltzer. New York, Boni-Liveright 1917. 61–70 **256**
Reprinted 1925, 82–95.

—— from *A sportsman's sketches.* In *The Warner library.* New York, Knickerbocker Press 1917. vol 25, 15082–090 **257**

—— from *A sportsman's sketches.* In *Great short stories of the world; an anthology selected from the literature of all periods and countries* ed Barrett Harper Clark and Maxim Lieber. New York, McBride 1925. 644–651 **258**

—— Tr Constance Garnett. In *Prose preferences* ed Sidney Cox and E. Freeman. New York, Harper 1926. 273–284 **259**

—— In *The world's one hundred best short stories* ed Grant Overton. New York, Funk-Wagnalls 1927. vol 4, 76–88 **260**

—— Tr Constance Garnett. In *The fifteen finest short stories* ed John Cournos. New York, Dodd-Mead 1928. 250–263 **261**

—— *Golden book magazine* XXII No 129 (Sep 1935) 301–306 **262**

—— In *The story survey* ed Harold Blodgett. Philadelphia, Lippincott 1939. **263**

—— *Encore* [Hoboken, N. J.] II No 8 (Sep 1942) 260–267 **264**

—— Tr Constance Garnett. In *A treasury of Russian life and humor* ed John Cournos. New York, Coward-McCann 1943. 219–226 **265**

—— In *A treasury of doctor stories by the world's great authors* ed Noah D. Fabricant and H. Werner. New York, Fell 1946. 201–210 **266**

—— In *Great short stories from the world's literature* ed Charles Neider. New York, Rinehart 1950. 468–477 **267**

"Foma, the wolf," In *World's great adventure stories.* New York, Black 1929. 203–209 **268**
"The bear."

"Hor and Kalinitch," In *The world's progress* vol IX. Chicago, The Delphian Society 1913. 488–501 **269**
Binder's title: *The Delphian course.*

"How Russians meet death," Tr Lady George Hamilton. *Temple bar* XLVIII (Dec 1876) 496–505 **270**
"Death."

"The living mummy," *Scribner's monthly* XII No 4 (Aug 1876) 563–569 **271**

"A living relic," Tr of "Zhivyye moshchi." *Scottish review* III (Dec 1884) 75–91 **272**
Reprinted in *Living Age* CLX No 2069 (Feb 16, 1884) 416–423.

—— from *A sportsman's sketches.* In *The Warner library.* New York, Knickerbocker Press 1917. vol 25, 15119–130 **273**

—— In *The Copeland translations* ed Charles T. Copeland. New York, Scribner 1934. 823–834 **274**

—— In *Modern short stories* ed Margaret E. Ashmun. New York, Macmillan 1941. 354–375 **275**

"Living relics," Tr Constance Garnett. In *A treasury of great Russian short stories; Pushkin to Gorky.* New York, Macmillan 1944. 215–227 **276**

"The raspberry water," In *Great stories of all nations* ed Maxim Lieber. New York, Brentano 1927. 751–759 **277**

"The rendezvous," Tr Herman Bernstein. In *Short story classics* ed William Patten. New York, Collier 1907. vol 1, 65–80 **278**

—— In *The masterpiece library of short stories* ed J. A. Hammerton. London, Educational Book Company 1920. vol 12, 117–124 **279**

—— *Golden book magazine* II No 11 (Nov 1925) 622–626 **280**

—— In *World's great romances.* New York, Black 1929. 337–343 **281**
See also "The tryst" (items 289–291).

"The singers," from *A sportsman's sketches.* In *The Warner library.* New York, Knickerbocker Press 1917. vol 25, 15107–118 **282**

—— In *The masterpiece library of short stories* ed J. A. Hammerton. London, Educational Book Company 1920. vol 12, 88–104 **283**

—— Tr Constance Garnett. In *A treasury of Russian short stories; Pushkin to Gorky* ed Avrahm Yarmolinsky. New York, Macmillan 1944. 90–106 **284**

—— Tr W. Morison. In *A first series of representative Russian stories, Pushkin to Gorky* ed Janko Lavrin. London, Westhouse 1946. 62–79 **285**

—— In *The heritage of European literature* ed Edward Howell Weatherly. Boston, Ginn 1948–49. vol 2, 492–501 **286**

—— In *Great Russian stories* comp Isai Kamen. New York, Random House 1959. 77–92. **287**

"Tatyana Borissovna and her Nephew," *Chautauquan* LIII No 3 (Feb 1909) 395–407 **288**

"The tryst," Tr Constance Garnett. In *An anthology of world prose* ed Carl van Doren. New York, Reynal Hitchcock 1935. 978–983 **289**

—— Tr Constance Garnett. In *A treasury of great Russian short stories; Pushkin to Gorky* ed Avrahm Yarmolinsky. New York, Macmillan 1944. 107–115 **290**

—— In *The heritage of European literature* ed Edward Howell Weatherly. Boston, Ginn 1948–49. vol 2, 501–506 **291**

"Yermolai and the miller's wife," Tr Constance Garnett. In *A treasury of short stories* ed Bernardine Kielty. New York, Simon Schuster 1947. 3–10 **292**

* * *

Spring floods. Tr Sophie Michell. *Eclectic magazine* Ns XVIII No 4 — XIX No 3 (Oct 1873 to Mar 1874) 436–449, 552–565, 686–699; 45–55, 177–187, 339–346 **293**

"The storm has passed," *Arena* II No 12 (Nov 1890) 705–706 **294**

"Strange adventure of Lieutenant Yergunof," *Galaxy* XXIX (1877) 459–475 **295**
Tr from the French.

"A strange story," Tr Edward Foord. *Eclectic magazine* Ns XL No 1 (July 1884) 98–108 **296**
Reprinted from *Merry England* II (1884).

—— Tr W. Morison. In *A first series of representative Russian stories, Pushkin to Gorky* ed Janko Lavrin. London, Westhouse 1946. 80–101 **297**

"Three meetings," Tr Agnes Lazarus. *Lippincott's magazine* XVI No 1 (Jul 1875) 21–35 **298**

"Three sketches: The museum. The kiss. A parting," Tr by H. Stewart. *Saturday review* CVIII No 2821 (Nov 20, 1909) 629–630 **299**
Reprinted in *Living age* CCLXIII No 3416 (Dec 25, 1909) 806–808. Not included in his *Collected Works* (Moscow 1954–58).

"Vassilissa," *Romance* III? (New York 1893) **300**

Vassilissa is the heroine of Turgenev's story, "Petushkov." Although the above cited publication has not been located, it is probably the same story as "Petushkov."

"Visions: A phantasy," *Galaxy* XIV No 1 (Jul 1872) 108–121 **301**

—— In *Library of choice literature.* Philadelphia, Gebbie 1888. vol 6, 42–47 **302**

—— In *The masterpiece library of short stories* ed J. A. Hammerton. London, Educational Book Company 1920. vol 12, 105–116 **303**

"The watch: an old man's story," *Lippincott's magazine* XVII (May 1876) 594–616 **304**

"The watch," In *The bridal march,* from the Norwegian of Bjornstjerne Bjornson, and *The watch,* from the Russian of Ivan Turgenieff. Tr J. Williams. London, Digby-Long 1893. 175 p **305**

"What Pushkin merits from Russia," Tr Elizabeth Brereton Lord. *Vassar review* No 38 (Feb 1937) p 14 **306**

"When I from thee was forced to part," *Arena* II No 12 (Nov 1890) p 706 **307**

"The wood lark," Tr Edna Underwood. In *The Slav anthology.* Portland, Me., Mosher Press 1931. 209–210 **308**

Works about Turgenev

[Mrs E Robinson. "Slavery in Russia"] *The North American review* LXXXII (Apr 1856) 293–318   **309**
    P 314–318 is a review of *Aus dem Tagebuche eines Jägers*, the 1850 German edition of *A sportsman's notebook*.

Athenaeum XXXVIII No 1781 (Dec 14, 1861) p 803   **310**
    Review of French edition of *A nest of gentlefolk*.

"A Russian romance," *Saturday review* XIII No 334 (Mar 22, 1862) 334–336   **311**
    Another review of the French edition of *A nest of gentlefolk*.

Athenaeum XLI No 1856 (May 23, 1863) 680–681   **312**
    Review of *Nouvelles Scènes de la Vie Russe; Elena; un Premier Amour*.

Saturday review XV No 399 (Jun 20, 1863) 799–800   **313**
    Review of French editions of *On the eve* and *First love*.

"A novel from Russian," *Nation* IV No 102 (Jun 13, 1867) 470–472   **314**
    Review of *Fathers and sons* (1867).

[C. E. Norton] *North American review* CV No 216 (Jul 1867) 328–329   **315**
    Review of Schuyler translation of *Fathers and sons* (1867).

"A Russian novel," *Saturday review* XXIV No 619 (Sep 7, 1867) 322–323   **316**
    Review of *Fathers and sons* (1867).

Athenaeum LI No 2119 (Jun 6, 1868) 789–790   **317**
    Review of *Smoke*.

"Iwan Turgenew, the Russian novelist," *The new eclectic* III (Dec 1868) 477–480   **318**
    Translated from the *Augsburger Allgemeine Zeitung*.

"Turguenief's novels," *North British review* L (Mar 1869) 22–64   **319**

"Liza," [review] *Saturday review* XXVIII No 718 (Jul 31, 1869) 163–164   **320**

[The Works of Ivan Sérguevitch Tourgéneff, Carlsruhe, Hasper 1866 — 5 v] *British quarterly review* L (Oct 1, 1869) 423–447   **321**
    Royal Gettmann attributes this unsigned article to C. E. Turner.

"M. Turguenief's 'Liza,'" *Every Saturday* VIII No 203 (Nov 20, 1869) 656–57   **322**
    Review of Ralston translation of *Liza*.

A. C. Dillmann. "Ivan Toorgenef, the novelist," *Lippincott's magazine* VII (May 1871) 494–502   **323**

[T. S. Perry] *Nation* XII No 307 (May 18, 1871) 340–341   **324**
    Review of *On the eve* (1871).

—— *Nation* XIV No 365 (Jun 27, 1872) 423–424   **325**
    Review of *Smoke* (1872).

[Eugene Schuyler] *Athenaeum* No 2331 (Jun 29, 1872) p 815   **326**
    Brief note on *Spring floods*.

[W. D. Howells] *Atlantic monthly* XXX No 178 (Aug 1872) 243–244   **327**
    Review of *Smoke* (1872).

[T. S. Perry] *Atlantic monthly* XXX No 181 (Nov 1872) p 630   **328**
    Review of German edition of *Spring floods*.

Atlantic monthly XXXI No 183 (Jan 1873) 110–112   **329**
    Review of *Drei Novellen* (Vienna 1872).

[W. D. Howells] *Atlantic monthly* XXXI No 184 (Feb 1873) 239–241   **330**
    Review of *Liza* (1872).

Hjalmar H. Boyesen. "A visit to Tourguéneff," *Galaxy* XVII (Apr 1874) 456–466   **331**

Henry James, Jr. [Iwan Turgéniew] *North American review* CXVIII No 243 (Apr 1874) 326–356   **332**
    Reprinted in *French poets and novelists*. London, Macmillan 1878, 1884, 1893, 1904, 1908, 1919. 211–252
    Also reprinted in *Partial portraits*. London, Macmillan 1888, 1894, 1899. 291–323

Thomas Sergeant Perry. "Ivan Turgénieff," *Atlantic monthly* XXXIII (May 1874) 565–575   **333**

[T. S. Perry] *Atlantic monthly* XXXV No 212 (Jun 1875) 748–749   **334**
    Review of *Skizzen aus dem Tagebuche eines Jägers*.

Athenaeum LXIX No 2573 (Feb 17, 1877) 217–218   **335**
    Review of Russian edition of *Virgin soil*.

"Notes," *Nation* xxiv No 608 (Feb 22, 1877) 117 **336**

　Brief paragraph discussing the English spelling of Turgenev's name, favoring Turgenef.

Henry James. "Ivan Turgenef's new novel," *Nation* xxiv No 617 (Apr 26, 1877) 252–253 **337**

　Review of 1877 French edition of *Virgin soil*.

[Hjalmar H. Boyesen] "Ivan Tourguéneff," *Scribner's monthly* xiv No 2 (May 1877) 200–207, port **338**

W. R. S. Ralston. "Russian revolutionary literature," *Nineteenth century* i (May 1877) 397–416 **339**

[T. S. Perry] *Atlantic monthly* xl No 237 (Jul 1877) 122–124 **340**

　Another review of the 1877 French *Virgin soil*.

T. E. Child. "Ivan Turgenieff," *Belgravia* xxxiii (Aug 1877) 212–223 **341**

Clara Barnes Martin. "Turgeneff and his translators," [Letter] *Nation* xxvi No 672 (May 16, 1878) 321–322 **342**

"Tourgénief's Virgin Soil," *Saturday review* xlv No 1183 (Jun 29, 1878) 830–831 **343**

　Review of Dilke's 1878 translation.

William L. Kingsley. "Nihilism in Russia as it appears in the novels of Ivan Turgenieff," *New Englander* xxxvii No 145 (Jul 1878) 553–572 **344**

Octave Thanet. "The moral purpose of Tourguéneff," *Journal of speculative philosophy* xii No 4 (Oct 1878) 427–434 **345**

S. E. Shevitch. "Russian novels and novelists of the day," *North American review* cxxviii No 268 (Mar 1879) 326–334 **346**

　Review of *Diary of a sportsman*, *Smoke*, and *Virgin soil*.

Clara Barnes Martin. "The greatest novelist's work for freedom," *Atlantic monthly* xliv. (Dec 1879) 761–770 **347**

Helen and Alice Zimmern. *Half-hours with foreign novelists*. vol II. London, Remington 1880. **348**

　Biographical sketch p 3–10. "The Nihilist" (p 10–34) from *Fathers and Sons*.

"Russia and nihilism in the novels of Tourgénieff," *Blackwood's magazine* cxxvii No 775 (May 1880) 623–647 **349**

Hjalmar H. Boyesen. "Tourguéneff and the nihilists," *Critic* i No 6 (Mar 26, 1881) 81–82 **350**

"Ivan Turguenief," *Saturday review* lii No 1356 (Oct 22, 1881) 509–510 **351**

Charles Edward Turner. "Tourgenieff's novels as interpreting the political movement in Russia," *Macmillan's magazine* xlv No 270 (Apr 1882) 471–486 **352**

"Ivan Surguéyevitch Tourguénief," *Athenaeum* lxxxii No 2915 (Sep 8, 1883) 305–306 **353**

"Ivan Turgénieff," *Saturday review* lvi No 1454 (Sep 8, 1883) p 306 **354**

[Memorial Notices] *Nation* xxxvii No 950 (Sep 13, 1883) p 230; No 958 (Nov 8, 1883) p 395 **355**

A. R. R. Barker. "Obituary. Ivan Turgenev," *Academy* xxiv No 593 (Sep 15, 1883) 179–180 **356**

W. R. S. Ralston. "Ivan Surguéyevitch Tourguénief," *Athenaeum* lxxxii No 2916 (Sep 15, 1883) 337–338 **357**

Hjalmar H. Boyesen. "Ivan Tourguéneff," *Critic* iii No 82 (Sep 22, 1883) 365–366 **358**

"Turgenieff [with] A Bibliography of Turgenieff," *The Literary world* xiv (Sep 22, 1883) 304–305 **359**

"Trollope and Turgenieff," *The Literary world* xiv (Oct 6 1883) p 327 **360**

　Reprinted from the *Athenaeum*.

"The funeral of Tourguenieff," *Saturday review* lvi No 1460 (Oct 20, 1883) 490–491 **361**

Alphonse Daudet. "Tourguéneff in Paris: Reminiscences by Daudet," *Century magazine* xxvii Ns v No 1 (Nov 1883) 48–53, port **362**

Bayard Tuckerman. "Ivan Sergheïevitch Turgeneff," *Princeton review* lix Ns xii (Nov 1883) 247–260 **363**

"Ivan Tourgénief," *Eclectic magazine* Ns xxxviii No 5 (Nov 1883) 643–649 **364**

　Reprints obituaries and memorials from the London *Spectator*, the London *Athenaeum*, and the *Saturday review*.

Henry James. "Ivan Turgénieff," *Atlantic monthly* liii No 315 (Jan 1884) 42–55 **365**

Wilbur Larremore. "Tourguéneff," *Overland monthly* 2nd ser iii No 3 (Mar 1884) 301–307 **366**

"Two of Turgenieff's tales," *Literary world* xv No 6 (Mar 22, 1884) p 87   **367**

   Review of 1884 Gersoni translation of *Mumu; and The diary of a superfluous man.*

Charlotte Adams. "Tourgueneff's youth," *Critic* v No 27 (Jul 5, 1884) 7–8   **368**

G. V. Staratsky. "Ivan Tourguénief," *Dublin review* xcv 3rd ser xii (Jul 1884) 46–65   **369**

"Ivan Serguievitch Tourgenieff," *London quarterly review* LXIII Ns III No 11 (Oct 1884) 38–55   **370**

   Review of *Tourgenieff's Novels, Liza,* etc.

William Richard Morfill. "The early life of Tourghéniev," *Academy* xxvi No 657 (Dec 6, 1884) 375–376   **371**

Clara Barnes Martin. "The mother of Turgeneff," *Atlantic monthly* LV No 329 (Mar 1885) 361–370   **372**

Arthur Tilley. "Ivan Turgénieff," *National review* iv No 23 (Jan 1885) 683–697; v No 30 (Aug 1885) 829–841   **373**

"Turgeneff in his letters," *Nation* XLI No 1053 (Sep 3, 1885) 190–192   **374**

Ernest Dupuy. *The great masters of Russian literature in the nineteenth century.* Tr Nathan Haskell Dole. New York, Crowell 1886. 117–213, port   **375**

[Isabel Florence Hapgood] "Tolstoi and Turgeneff," *Nation* XLII No 1088 (May 6, 1886) 388–389   **376**

   Review of *Anna Karénina.*

W. H. Allen. "A Russian fury," *Cosmopolitan* II No 2 (Oct 1886) 76–84   **377**

   Popular article on Turgenev's mother.

[F. Bôcher] "Russian authors for French readers," *Nation* XLIII No 1111 (Oct 14, 1886) 312–313   **378**

Eugene Melchoir Marie de Vogue. *The Russian novelists.* Tr Jane Loring Edmonds. Boston, Lothrop 1887. 88–140   **379**

Thomas Sergeant Perry. "Russian novels," *Scribner's magazine* I No 2 (Feb 1887) 252–256   **380**

Joel Benton. "The Russian novel," *Southern Bivouac* v (Louisville, May 1887) 723–725 **381**

Harriet Waters Preston. "The spell of the Russian writers," *Atlantic monthly* LX (Aug 1887) 199–213   **382**

George Moore. "Turgeneff," *Fortnightly review* XLIX Ns XLIII (Feb 1, 1888) 237–251   **383**

"Two Russian realists," [Dostoyevsky and Tolstoy] *London quarterly review* LXX Ns X (Apr 1888) 56–73. See p 56–57   **384**

Georg Brandes. *Impressions of Russia.* Tr from the Danish by S. C. Eastman. New York, Crowell 1889. 271–300   **385**

   An 1888 ed is mentioned in the preface.

——— New York, Crowell 1899.   **386**

Ivan Panin. *Lectures on Russian literature: Pushkin, Gogol, Turgenef, Tolstoy.* New York, Putnam 1889. 115–153   **387**

Emilia Pardo-Bazán. *Russia, its people and its literature.* Tr from the Spanish by F. Gardiner. Chicago, McClurg 1890. 209–233   **388**

Roman I. Zubof. "Tourgenief and the Russian social problem," *New England magazine* Ns I No 6 (Feb 1890) 702–708   **389**

Charles Johnston. "The quarrel between Turgeniev and Tolstoi," *Academy* XXXVIII No 965 (Nov 1, 1890) 392–393   **390**

Nathan Haskell Dole. "Turgénief as a poet," *Arena* II No 12 (Nov 1890) 688–707   **391**

   Excerpts from "A visitation."

Leopold Katscher. "Tourgenieff in his letters," *Universal review* VIII No 32 (Dec 15, 1890) 577–596   **392**

George Moore. "Turgeneff," In *Impressions and opinions.* New York, Scribner 1891. 65–97   **393**

——— New York, Brentano 1913. 44–65   **394**

"Russia: its people and government," *Quarterly review* CLXXII No 343 (Jan 1891) 113–142 **395**

   Review of French edition of *Fathers and Sons.*

Allan Monkhouse. "Turgenieff," In *Books and plays.* London, Mathews-Lane 1894. 118–154   **396**

Hjalmar Hjorth Boyesen. "The mother of Ivan Tourguéneff," *Century magazine* XLVIII No 2 (Jun 1894) 249–252   **397**

Nathan Haskell Dole. "An episode in Turgénief's life," *Arena* X No 57 (Aug 1894) 401–408   **398**

William D. Howells. *My literary passions.* New York, Harper 1895. 229–232   **399**

[William D. Howells] "Mr Howells on Tourgueneff," *Critic* XXVI No 682 (Mar 16, 1895) 204–205 ***400***
From *The Ladies Home Journal.*

Reginald George Burton. "An appreciation of Russian fictional literature," *Westminster review* CXLIV No 5 (Nov 1895) 539–544 ***401***

Edward Arthur Brayley Hodgetts. "Turgueniev's place in literature," *Anglo-Russian literary society proceedings* No 13 (Jan–Mar 1896) p 13 ***402***

Maurice Todhunter. "Ivan Turgenev," *Westminster review* CXLVI No 2 (Aug 1896) 141–149 ***403***

Gertrude Shepherd. "Observations on some of the women of Turgueniev," *Anglo-Russian literary society proceedings* No 17 (1897) 68–79 ***404***

Serge Mikhailovich Volkonski. *Pictures of Russian history and Russian literature.* Boston, Lamson-Wolffe 1897. 249–256 ***405***

—— London 1897. ***406***

—— Boston, Lamson-Wolffe 1898. 249–256 ***407***

William D. Howells. "My favorite novelist and his best book," *Munsey's magazine* XVII No 1 (Apr 1897) 18–25 ***408***

F. Volkhovsky. "Ivan S. Turgenev," *Free Russia* IX No 4 (1898) 26–29 ***409***

Virginia M. Crawford. *Studies in foreign literature.* London, Duckworth 1899. 7–18 ***410***
Reprinted 1908.

Eugene Melchoir de Vogue. "Russian literature; its great period and its great novelists," In *Universal anthology* XVII (1899) xxxi–xlix ***411***

Georg Brandes. "Nihilist circles in Russia," Tr by S. C. Eastman. In *Universal anthology* XXXI (1899) 340–349 ***412***
Reprinted from his *Impressions of Russia*, item 385.

E. A[rnold] B[ennett] "Ivan Turgenev, an enquiry," *Academy* LVII No 1435 (Nov 4, 1899) 514–517, port ***413***

Kazimierz Waliszewski. *A history of Russian literature.* London, Heinemann; New York, Appleton 1900. 278–298 ***414***

—— New York, Appleton 1905. 278–298 ***415***

—— New York, Appleton 1927. 278–298 ***416***

"Ivan Turgenev," *Literature* VI No 126 (Mar 17, 1900) 219–220; No 128 (Mar 31, 1900) p 256 ***417***
I The Controversialist
II The Artist

Eugene Schuyler. *Selected essays.* New York, Scribner 1901. 259–274, passim ***418***

Isabel Florence Hapgood. *A survey of Russian literature, with selections.* New York, Chautauqua Press 1902. 164–180 ***419***

Charles Whibley. "Ivan Turgenev," *North American review* CLXXIV No 543 (Feb 1902) 212–221 ***420***

George Moore. "Avowals, being the second of a new series of 'Confessions of a young man,'" [Balzac and Turgenev] *Lippincott's monthly magazine* LXXII No 16 (Oct 1903) 481–488 ***421***

James Gibbons Huneker. *Overtones; A book of temperaments.* New York, Scribner 1904. 142–161 ***422***

—— New York, Scribner 1912. 142–161 ***423***

William Leonard Courtney. "Turgenieff," In *Development of Maurice Maeterlinck and other sketches of foreign writers.* London, Richards 1904. ***424***
Chapter 5.

"Turgeneff and his translators," *Nation* LXXVIII No 2014 (Feb 4, 1904) 93–95 ***425***
Review of the Garnett and Hapgood collected editions.

Piotr Alekseyevich Kropotkin. *Russian literature.* New York, McClure-Phillips 1905. 89–109, passim ***426***
Reissued as *Ideals and realities in Russian literature.* New York, Knopf 1909 (q.v.). This title was reprinted by Knopf in 1915. All have the same pagination.

"A glance backward at Ivan Turgenieff and his work," *Critic* XLVI No 5 (May 1905) 444–447 ***427***

"Turgenev and the golden era of Russian literature," *American monthly review of reviews* XXXV No 6 (Jun 1907) 741–742 ***428***

[Lady] Anne Thackeray Ritchie. "Concerning Tourguénieff," *New quarterly* I No 2 (Mar 1908) 181–194 ***429***
Reprinted in *Living age* CLVII No 3329 (Apr 25, 1908) 214–220, and in *Blackstick Papers*, 1908.

"Turgénieff, 'The greatest of all novelists,'" *Current literature* XLIII No 2 (Aug 1907) 174–178 **430**
    Review of the Garnett and Hapgood translations and a French biography.

Crossfield, H. "Turgueneff's novels and the Russian revolution," *Westminster review* CLXVIII No 5 (Nov 1907) 523–536 **431**

Simeon Strunsky. "Turgenieff and the moderns," *Nation* LXXXV No 2213 (Nov 28, 1907) 488–490 **432**
    A review of the Hapgood collected edition.

"Turgénieff anew," *Atlantic monthly* C (Dec 1907) 862–863 **433**

Alexander Brückner. *A literary history of Russia.* Ed by E. H. Minns and trans from the German by H. Havelock. London, Unwin 1908. 338–357 **434**

Maurice Baring. "Tolstoy and Turgenev," *Quarterly review* CXI No 420 (Jul 1909) 180–202 **435**
    Review of Garnett's Heinemann edition of *The works of I. S. Turgenev* (item 2).

Maurice Baring. *Landmarks in Russian literature.* New York, Macmillan 1910. **436**
    Ch 4: "Tolstoy and Turgenev" 77–115
    Ch 5: "The Place of Turgenev" 116–124

Jacob Tonson. "Books and persons," [Turgenev and Dostoyevsky] *New Age* Ns VI No 22 (Mar 31, 1910) 518–519 **437**

Francis Gribble. "Tourgueneff," *Fortnightly review* XCIII Ns LXXXVII (Jun 1910) 1071–81 **438**

Richard H. P. Curle. "Tourgeneff and the life-illusion," *Fortnightly review* XCIII Ns LXXXVII (Jun 1910) 1082–89 **439**

"Turgenieff and the woman he loved," *Current literature* IL No 2 (Aug 1910) 213–215 **440**

Ford Madox Ford. *The critical attitude.* London, Duckworth 1911. 156–160 **441**
    In chapter on "The Woman of the Novelists."
    Reprinted 1915.

John Arthur Thomas Lloyd. *Two Russian reformers: Ivan Turgenev, Leo Tolstoy.* New York, London, Lane 1911. 335 p, ports **442**
    Review: George Sampson. "Tolstoy and another," *Bookman* XXXIX No 232 (Jan 1911) 189–190.

William Lyon Phelps. *Essays on Russian novelists.* New York, Macmillan 1911. 62–129 bibliog 285–322 **443**
    Reprinted 1917.

Nevill Forbes. "Turgenev," *Russian review* I No 3 (London 1912) 116–140 **444**

W[illiam] D. H[owells] and T[homas] S[ergeant] P[erry] "Recent Russian fiction; a conversation," *North American review* CXCVI No 680 (Jul 1912) 85–103 **445**

Philip Stafford Moxom. "Turgenief: The man," *North American review* CXCVI No 682 (Sep 1912) 394–405 **446**
    Reprinted in *Two Masters, Browning and Turgenev.* Boston, Sherman-French 1912.

Eugène Melchoir Marie de Vogüe. *The Russian novel.* Tr from the 11th French ed by H. A. Sawyer. London, Chapman-Hall 1913. 155–203, ports **447**

John Cournos. "Turgenev, the emancipator," *Lippincott's monthly magazine* XCI No 9 (Feb 1913) 233–238 **448**
    Reprints "The district doctor," p 239–246.

Maurice Baring. *An outline of Russian literature.* London, Williams-Norgate 1914–15. 161–175 **449**

Count Ilya Tolstoy. "Reminiscences of Tolstoy," Tr George Calderon. *Century magazine* LXXXVIII No 3 (Jul 1914) 424–428 **450**

Leo Wiener. *An interpretation of the Russian people.* New York, McBride, Nast 1915. passim **451**

Padraic Colum. "Maria Edgeworth and Ivan Turgenev," *British review* XI No 1 (Jul 1915) p 109 **452**

Henry St. George Tucker. "A Russian novelist's estimate of the Russian intellectual," *Sewanee review* XXIV No 1 (Jan 1916) 61–68 **453**

Arnold Bennett. *Books and persons.* London, Chatto & Windus 1917. 208–213 **454**

Edward Garnett. *Turgenev; a study.* With foreword by Joseph Conrad. London, Collins 1917. 206 p, port (Kings' Way classics) **455**

Henry James. "Ivan Turgeneff," *The Warner library.* vol 25. New York, Knickerbocker Press 1917. 15057–62 **456**

Radoslav Andrea Tsanoff. "The art of Ivan Turgenev," In *The problem of life in the Russian novel; five public lectures. . . .* Houston, Rice Institute Apr 1917. 144–179 (Rice Institute pamphlets vol 4) **457**

[List of references on Ivan Sergieevich Turgenev] Washington, Library of Congress 1917. ff 4. **458**
    Cited in Bestermann. Unlocated.

"Turgenef's failure," *Literary digest* LIX No 6 (Nov 9, 1918) p 28 **459**

Humphry Sandwich. "Hamlet the lover: thoughts on Ivan Turgeniev's essay 'Hamlet and Don Quixote,'" *Anglo-Russian Literary society proceedings* No 85 (1919) 33–41 **460**
Discussion, 41–43.

Robert Lynd. *Old and new masters.* New York, Scribner 1919. 117–122 **461**

John Arthur Thomas Lloyd. "The charm of Turgenev," *Fortnightly review* CXII Ns CVI (Aug 1, 1919) 297–307 **462**

A. Clutton-Brock. *Essays on books.* New York, Dutton; London, Methuen 1920. 157–168 **463**
Reprinted from *Times Literary Supplement.*

Moissaye J. Olgin. *A guide to Russian literature, 1820–1917.* New York, Harcourt-Brace-Howe 1920. 76–81 **464**

Joseph Conrad. *Notes on life and letters.* London, Dent 1921. 61–65 **465**

—— New York, Doubleday 1921. 45–48 **466**

Percy Lubbock. *The craft of fiction.* London, Cape 1921. 121–122 **467**
Reprinted in *The Travellers' library* series 1926, 1928, 1929, 1932, 1935, 1939.

Shakhnovski. *A short history of Russian literature.* Tr Serge Tomkeyeff. London, Paul-Trench-Trubner 1921. 127–129 **468**

Stuart P. B. Mais. *Why we should read* — London, Grant Richards 1921. 263–269 **469**

Jacob Zeitlin. "Turgenev and his heroes," *Nation* CXII No 2915 (May 18, 1921) 712–713 **470**

Lilian Rowland-Brown. "Turgenev and girlhood," *Nineteenth century* XC No 534 (Aug 1921) 230–244 **471**

M. P. Willcocks. "Turgenev," *English review* XXXIII No 2 (Aug 1921) 175–189 **472**
Reprinted in *Between the old world and the new.* London, Allen-Unwin 1925; New York, Stokes 1926.

Oliver M. Sayler. "Turgenieff as a playwright," *North American review* CCXIV No 790 (Sep 1921) 393–400 **473**

Sarah F. Radoff. "The intellectualist in Strindberg and Turgeniev," *Texas review* VII No 3 (1922) 215–235 **474**

Alexander Kaun. "Turgenev rerambled," *Bookman* LV (May 1922) 308–311 **475**

"A fortuitous advantage," [Gogol's *Dead souls* and Turgenev's *Sportsman's sketches*] *Freeman* VII No 169 (Jun 6, 1923) 294–295 **476**

M. O. Gershenson. "A sketch of Turgenev," *Living age* CCCXVIII No 4132 (Sep 15, 1923) 513–516 **477**
First English translation of article in *Neue Zürcher Zeitung* (Jul 31, 1923) from his *Mechta i mysl' I. S. Turgeneva* [Dreams and thoughts of Turgenev] Moscow 1919.

Frank Harris. "Ivan Turgenief: A snapshot," In *Contemporary portraits.* Fourth series. London, Richards 1924. 49–53 **478**

Konstantin Sergeyevich Stanislavski. *My life in art.* Tr by J. J. Robbins. Boston, Little-Brown 1924. 542–546, passim **479**

Leo Wiener. *The contemporary drama of Russia.* Boston, Little-Brown 1924. 276 p **480**
See index and bibliography.

Prince D. S. Mirsky [Dmitrii Petrovich Svyatopolk-Mirski] *Modern Russian literature.* London, Oxford Univ Press 1925. 22–33, port. **481**

Abraham Yarmolinsky. *Turgenev, the man — his art — and his age.* New York, Century 1926. 386 p, ports **482**

—— London, Hodder & Stoughton 1927. **483**
See also 1959 edition.

Lawrence F. Abbott. "A word about Russia," *Outlook* [New York] CXLIII No 8 (Jun 23, 1926) 275–276 **484**

[Turgenev the modern] *Theatre Arts monthly* X No 11 (Nov 1926) 725–727 **485**

Janko Lavrin. *Russian literature.* London, Benn [1927] 38–41 biblio (Benn's Sixpenny Library No 56) **486**

John Galsworthy. "Six novelists in profile," in *Castles in Spain and other screeds.* London, Heinemann 1927. p 150–153 on Turgenev. **487**
Same address reprinted in *Candelabra*, another collection of essays and addresses. London, Heinemann 1932. 124–127.

Prince D. S. Mirsky [Dmitrii Petrovich Svyatopolk-Mirski] *A history of Russian literature, from the earliest times to the death of Dostoyevsky.* London, Routledge 1927. 236–254, passim **488**
Included in *A history of Russian literature* (1949), item 540.

Arnold Bennett. *The savour of life.* New York, Doubleday, Doran 1928. 127–135 **489**

WORKS ABOUT TURGENEV

Frank Swinnerton. *A London bookman.* London, Secker 1928. 205–208 **490**

Edmund Gosse. "A memory of Tourgenieff," *London mercury* XVII No 100 (Feb 1928) p 403 **491**

Joshua Kunitz. *Russian literature and the Jew.* New York, Columbia Univ Press 1929. 46–51, passim **492**
    Columbia University PhD thesis. Short discussion of "The Jew."

Item not used **493**

Janko Lavrin. *Studies in European literature.* London, Constable 1929. 58–79 **494**

E. H. Carr. "Turgenev and Dostoyevsky," *Slavonic review* VIII No 22 (Jun 1929) 156–163 **495**

Gustave Flaubert. "Letters to Turgenev," *Living age* CCCXXXVII No 4349 (Nov 1, 1929) 295–299 **496**

E. H. Carr. "Two Russians," *Fortnightly review* CXXXII (Dec 2, 1929) 823–826 **497**

Cornelia Pulsifer Kelley. *The early development of Henry James.* In *Studies in language and literature* XV No 1–2. Urbana, Illinois University (May–February) 1930. See index **498**

William Lyon Phelps. "Turgenev, ancestor: The Russian novelist as a source of modern psychological drama," *Theatre Guild magazine* VII No 8 (May 1930) 37–39, illus **499**

Catherine Radziwill. "Ivan Turgenev," *Commonweal* XIV No 15 (Aug 12, 1931) 361–362 **500**

Clarence A. Manning. "Ivan Sergyeyevich Turgenev," *South Atlantic quarterly* XXX No 4 (Oct 1931) 366–381 **501**

Harry Hershkowitz. *Democratic ideas in Turgenev's works.* New York, Columbia Univ Press 1932. 131 p, biblio **502**
    Columbia Univ thesis, published in the series, Columbia University Slavonic Studies.

E. A. Osborne. "Russian literature and translations: Ivan Sergeevich Turgenev, 1818–1883," *Bookman* LXXXIII (Dec 1932) 198–202. port **503**

Alexander Kaun. "Turgenev, the European," *Books abroad* VII (Jul 1933) 274–277, port p 270 **504**

Edward Bernstein. "Turgenev and the Tolstoys," *New statesman and nation* VII (Mar 10, 1934) 349–350 **505**

Sophie Andreyevna Tolstoy (Bers). "Tolstoy versus Turgeniev: The childish quarrel between two literary giants that almost ended in a duel, narrated by Tolstoy's wife," *Golden Book magazine* XX No 115 (Jul 1934) 91–92 **506**

Virginia Woolf. "The novels of Turgenev," *Yale review* XXIII No 2 (Winter 1934) 276–283 **507**
    Reprinted in *The Captain's Death Bed and other essays.* New York, Harcourt-Brace, 1950. 53–61.

Ford Madox Ford. "Turgenev, the beautiful genius," *American Mercury* XXXIX No 153 (Sep 1936) 41–50 **508**

—— *Portraits from life.* Boston, Houghton-Mifflin 1937. 143–163 **509**

—— London, Allen-Unwin 1938, under title *Mightier than the sword.* 190–214. See also p 30. **510**
    Reprinted from *American Mercury* XXXIX No 153 (Sep 1936) 41–50 (item 508).

Nicolas E. Niewiadomsky. "Master of Language," [Letter] *American Mercury* XL No 158 (Feb 1937) p 252 **511**
    Rebuttal by Ford Madox Ford on same page.

V. S. Pritchett. "A hero of our time?" *London Mercury* XXXVI No 216 (Aug 1937) 359–364 **512**

Ivar Spector. *The golden age of Russian literature.* Seattle, University Book Store 1938. mimeo 49–71, biblio **513**

—— Los Angeles, Cal., Scholastic Press 1939. 75–103 **514**

—— Rev ed, Caldwell, Idaho, Caxton Printers 1943. ports. 75–103 **515**

Royal Alfred Gettmann. *Turgenev in England and America.* Urbana, Univ of Illinois Press 1941. 196 p (Illinois studies in language and literature XXVII No 2) biblio 187–194 **516**

Daniel Lerner. "The influence of Turgenev on Henry James," *Slavonic and East European review* XX No 1 (Dec 1941) 28–54 **517**

Janko Lavrin. *An introduction to the Russian novel.* London, Methuen 1942. 57–66 **518**

John Arthur Thomas Lloyd. *Ivan Turgenev, a literary biography.* London, Hale 1942. 227 p, ports **519**

—— London, Hale; New York, Transatlantic Arts; Toronto, Ryerson Press 1943. **520**

V. S. Pritchett. "Books in general," *New statesman and nation* Ns XXIII No 569 (Jan 17, 1942) p 43; Ns XXXVI No 920 (Oct 23, 1948) p 351; Ns XLVII No 1203 (Mar 27, 1954) 409–410 **521**

Raymond Mortimer. "Books in general," *New Statesman and Nation* Ns XXVI No 646 (Jul 10, 1943) p 27; Ns XXVI No 651 (Aug 14, 1943) p 107 **522**

Charles Morgan. *Reflections in a mirror.* First series. London, Macmillan 1944. 165–173 **523**

Noel Annan. "Novelist-philosophers III: Turgenev," *Horizon* XI No 63 (Mar 1945) 152–163 **524**

George Halperin. *Tolstoy, Dostoevski, Turgenev; The three great men in Russia's world of literature.* Chicago, Chicago Literary Club 1946. 73 p **525**

V. S. Pritchett. "The Russian day," *The living novel.* London, Chatto-Windus 1946. 219–225 **526**

Valentine Snow. *Russian writers; a bio-bibliographical dictionary. From the age of Catherine II to the October revolution of 1917.* vol I. New York, International Book Service 1946. 197–202 **527**

William Henry Chamberlin. "Turgenev: The eternal romantic," *Russian review* v No 2 (Spring 1946) 10–23 **528**

Nicholas N. Sergievsky. "The tragedy of a great love: Turgenev and Pauline Viardot," *American Slavic and East European review* v No 14–15 (Nov 1946) 55–71 **529**

Amrei Ettlinger and Joan M. Gladstone. *Russian literature, theatre and art; a bibliography of works in English, published 1900–1945.* London, Hutchinson 1947. 86–88 **530**

Helen Muchnic. *An introduction to Russian literature.* Garden City, NY, Doubleday 1947. 125–149 **531**

Richard Hare. *Russian literature from Pushkin to the present day.* London, Methuen 1947. 63–77 **532**

Varvara, Nikolayevna Zhitova. *The Turgenev family.* Tr by A. S. Mills. London, Harvill Press 1947. 179 p **533**

    First published in *Vestnik yevropy,* Nov–Dec 1884.

—— New York, Roy Publishers 1954? **534**

Henry James. *The art of fiction, and other essays.* Intro by Morris Roberts. New York, Oxford Univ Press 1948. **535**

    Includes two essays on Turgenev, one a reprint from the *North American review.*

Janko Lavrin. *From Pushkin to Mayakovsky, a study in the evolution of a literature.* London, Sylvan Press 1948. 104–122, passim **536**

Lord David Cecil. "Turgenev," *Fortnightly* CLXIV (1948) 42–49 **537**

    Reprinted in *Virginia quarterly review* XXIV (1948) 591–601.

Walter A. Strauss. "Turgenev in the role of publicity agent for Flaubert's *La Tentation de Saint Antoine,*" *Harvard Library Bulletin* II No 3 (Autumn 1948) 405–410 **538**

Lord David Cecil. *Poets and story-tellers; a book of critical essays.* London, Constable 1949. 123–138 **539**

Prince D. S. Mirsky [Dmitrii Petrovich Svyatopolk-Mirski] *A history of Russian literature.* Ed and abridged by Francis J. Whitfield. New York, Knopf 1949. 139–140, 184–198, 233–234, passim **540**

Henry Gifford. *The hero of his time; a theme in Russian literature.* London, Longmans 1950. 141–148, 158–176 et passim **541**

F. W. J. Hemmings. *The Russian novel in France 1884–1914.* London, Oxford Univ Press 1950. 20–24, 31–38 et passim **542**

Mark L'vovich Slonim. *The epic of Russian literature, from its origins through Tolstoy.* New York, Oxford Univ Press 1950. 250–271 **543**

Charles Morgan. "Turgenev's treatment of a love-story," *Transactions of the Royal Society of literature of the United Kingdom* Ns XXV (1950) 102–119 **544**

Zbigniew Folejewski. "Turgenev and Prus," *Slavonic and East European review* XXIX (Dec 1950) 132–138 **545**

Boris V. Varneke. *History of the Russian theatre.* Tr Boris Brasol. New York, Macmillan 1951. 400–406 et passim **546**

David Footman. "Turgenev rediscovered," *Listener* XLV (Apr 5, 1951) 546–547 **547**

Renato Poggioli. "Realism in Russia," *Comparative literature* III No 3 (Summer 1951) 253–267 **548**

David Garnett. "Turgenev, Madame Viardot, and *A Month in the Country,*" *Adelphi* XXVII No 4 (Third quarter 1951) 346–350 **549**

Nina Brodianski. "Turgenev's short stories. A revaluation," *Slavonic and East European review* xxxii No 78 (Dec 1953) 70–91 **550**

David Magarshack. *Turgenev; a life.* London, Faber 1954. ports. biblio, 314–316 **551**
  Review: Ivar Spector, *Russian review* xiv No 3 (Apr 1955) 163–164.

Dorothy Brewster. *East-West passage; a study in literary relationships.* London, Allen-Unwin 1954. 219–226, passim **552**
  Review: René Wellek, *Russian review* xiv No 3 (Jul 1955) 267–268.

Janko Lavrin. *Russian writers; their lives and literature.* New York, Van Nostrand 1954. 116–131 et passim port **553**
  Review: Marc Slonim, *Russian review* xiv No 1 (Jan 1955) 75–76.

Alfred Kazin. "Turgenev and the non-Russians," In *The inmost leaf.* New York, Harcourt, Brace 1955. 89–92 **554**

—— New York, Noonday Press 1959. 89–92 (Noonday paperbacks)

Dmytro Chyzhevs'kyi. "Manuscripts of Dostoevsky and Turgenev at Harvard," *Harvard library bulletin* ix (1955) 410–415 **555**

Harold Orel. "English critics and the Russian novel, 1850–1917," *Slavonic and East European review* xxxiii No 81 (Jun 1955) 457–469 **556**

Gilbert Phelps. *The Russian novel in English fiction.* London, Hutchinson 1956. 42–138 et passim **557**

Wacław Lednicki. *Bits of table talk on Pushkin, Mickiewicz, Goethe, Turgenev, and Sienkiewicz.* The Hague, Nijhoff 1956. 62–86 et passim (International Scholars Forum V) **558**

Oscar Cargill. "The Princess Casamassima; a critical reappraisal," *PMLA* lxxi No 1 (Mar 1956) 97–117 **559**

Mildred A. Martin. "The last shall be first; a study of three Russian short stories . . . Turgenev's 'Biryuk,'" *Bucknell review* vi No 1 (Mar 1956) 13–23 **560**

Irving Howe. "Turgenev, the virtues of hesitation," *Hudson review* viii No 4 (Winter 1956) 533–551 **561**

Ralph E. Matlaw. "Turgenev's art in *Spring Torrents,*" *Slavonic and East European review* xxxv No 84 (Dec 1956) 157–171 **562**

Henry James. "Ivan Turgenev's *Virgin Soil,*" In *Literary reviews and essays* ed Albert Mordell. New York, Twayne 1957. 190–196 **563**

Isaiah Berlin. "An episode in the life of Ivan Turgenev," *London magazine* iv No 7 (1957) 14–18 **564**
  Following this short article Turgenev's "A Fire at Sea" is reprinted. See item 144.

Ralph E. Matlaw. "Turgenev's novels: civic responsibility and literary predilection," *Harvard Slavic studies* iv (1957) 249–262 **565**

Edmund Wilson. "Turgenev and the life-giving drop," *New Yorker* xxxiii (Oct 19, 1957) 163–216 **566**
  Reprinted in Turgenev's *Literary reminiscences and autobiographical fragments* tr by David Magarshak. See item 18, p 3–64.

E. D. Goy. "The attitude of the Serbs to Turgenev's works in the 19th century," *Slavonic and East European review* xxxvi No 86 (Dec 1957) 123–149 **567**

Cyril Bryner. "Turgenev and the English speaking world," In *Three papers in Slavonic studies* (Fourth International Congress of Slavists. Moscow 1958) Vancouver, Univ of British Columbia 1958. 3–19 **568**

Marc Slonim. *An outline of Russian literature.* London, Oxford Univ Press 1958. 89–98 et passim **569**

New York Public Library. Slavonic Division. "Ivan Sergeyevich Turgenev, 1818–1883." **570**
  Unpublished exhibition material from the 75th anniversary exhibit in 1958.

Prince D. S. Mirsky [Dmitrii Petrovich Svyatopolk-Mirski] *A history of Russian literature from the beginning to 1900.* New York, Vintage Books 1958. 193–208 et passim **571**

Ralph E. Matlaw. "A New Letter of Turgenev," *Harvard Library bulletin* xii No 2 (Spring 1958) 268–270 **572**

Karol Maichel. "The collected works of Russian classical authors," *American Slavic and East European review* xvii No 2 (Apr 1958) 223–225 **573**

Sergei Bertensson. "Turgenev and Savina," *American Slavic and East European review* xvii (Dec 1958) 530–533 **574**

Abraham Yarmolinsky. *Turgenev: the man, his art and his age.* New York, Orion Press 1959; London, Deutsch, Toronto, Burns & MacEachern 1960. 406 p illus   **575**

——— New York, Colliers books 1961. 362 p   **575A**

    Review: Richard Gilman, *Commonweal* LXX No 18 (Aug 28, 1959) 451–452.

Richard Hare. *Portraits of Russian personalities between reform and revolution.* London, Oxford Univ Press 1959. 68–103   **576**

V. S. Pritchett. "The marksman," *New Statesman* LVII (1959) 74–75   **577**

Oscar Mandel. "Molière and Turgenev: the literature of no-judgment," *Comparative literature* XI No 3 (Summer 1959) 233–249   **578**

Milton Hindus. "The duels in Mann and Turgenev," *Comparative literature* XI No 4 (Fall 1959) 308–312   **579**

Richard Freeborn. *Turgenev; the novelist's novelist.* London, Oxford Univ Press 1960. 201 p   **580**

Richard George Kappler. [Turgenev and the French] Diss, Columbia Univ 1960. 195 p microfilm   **581**

"Quixotic Hamlet," *MD, Medical newsmagazine* v No 2 (Feb 1961) 180–191   **582**

Title Index

Numbers refer to items, not pages. Items with asterisks represent transliterated Russian titles of Turgenev's works for which no translations have been found. An English title entry is followed by the equivalent Russian title [in square brackets]. A Russian title entry is followed by all English variant titles (in parentheses) and their item numbers. Item numbers in italics refer to reviews.

* A. N. Khovrinoĭ
Abide 89 [Stoĭ!]
About nightingales 18 [O Solov'yakh]
Accept the verdict of fools ... 231 [Uslyshish' sud gluptza]
Acia 3, 27 [Asya]
The adventure of second lieutenant Bubnov 115 [Pokhozhdeniya podporuchika Bubnova]
The adversary 231 [Sopernik]
After death 116 [Posle smerti] *See also* Klara Milich
The agent 3, 4 [Burmistr]
Alms 88, 89, 91, 231 [Milostynya]
An amicable settlement 23 [Zavtrak u predvoditelva]
Andreĭ Kolosov 3, 4, 5
* Andreĭ; poéma
Annals of a sportsman 1 [Zapiski okhotnika]
Annouchka 30 [Asya]
The antchar 117 [Zatish'ye]
Apropos of "Fathers and Children" 18, 118 [Po povodu "Ottzov i deteĭ"]
The assignation 95 [Svidaniye]
Assja 119 [Asya]
Asya 4, 5, 24, 28, 29, 119, 120 (Acia 3, 27; Annouchka 30; Assja; Assya)
Author and critic 91 [Pisatel' i kritik]
Autumn 121, 122 [Osen']
* Avtobiografiya
An axiom 88 [Zhiteĭskoye pravilo]
The azure realm 4 [Lazurnoye tzarstvo]

A baby's cry 91 [U-a ... U-a ...]
The bachelor 23, 31 [Kholostyak]
The bailiff 102 [Burmistr]
Ballada 123
The banquet of the deity 231 [Pir u verkhovnovo sushchestva]
The banquet of the supreme being 91 [Pir u verkhovnovo sushchestva]
The bear 102 [Biryuk]
Beejina Lough 95 [Bezhin lug]
The beggar 88–91, 231 [Nishchiĭ]
Beneficence and gratitude 124 [Pir u verkhovnovo sushchestva]
Bez gnezda (A bird without a nest 91)
Bezdenezh'ye (Broke 23)
Bezhin lug (Beejina Lough 95; Bezhin meadow 24, 32, 65, 102, 245, 246; Byezhin meadow 4, 250; Byezhin prairie 3, 251)

Bezhin meadow 24, 32, 65, 102, 245, 246 [Bezhin lug]
* Bezlunnaya noch'
A bird without a nest 91 [Bez gnezda]
Biryuk 3, 65, 86, 247–249 (The bear 102; Foma the bireouk 95; Foma, the wolf 12, 268; The wolf 4)
The blackbird 91 [Drozd]
Bliznetzy (The twins 91)
The blockhead 88, 89, 200, 231 [Durak]
The Borzoi Turgenev 11
The bourmister 95 [Burmistr]
The Brahmin 91 [Bramin]
Bramin (The Brahmin 91)
Bretior (The bully 4, 5, 126; The duellist 3; The ruffian 9)
The brigadier 3–5, 7, 9, 125 [Brigadir]
Broke 23 [Bezdenezh'ye]
Brozhu nad ozerom ... tumanny (I wander round the lake 157)
The bully 4, 5, 126 [Bretior]
Burmistr (The agent 3, 4; The bailiff 102; The bourmister 95; The children of the czar 241; The steward 65)
Byezhin meadow 4, 250 [Bezhin lug]
Byezhin prairie 3, 251 [Bezhin lug]
* Byloye schast'ye

Cabbage-soup 88–91, 201, 202, 231 [Shchi]
Carelessness 23 [Neostorozhnost']
Charity 90 [Milostynya]
Chasy (The watch 3–5, 304, 305)
* Chelovek, kakikh mnogo
Chelovek v seykh ochkakh (Monsieur François 180; The man in the grey spectacles 18)
Cherepa (The skulls 88–91, 231)
Chernorabochiĭ i beloruchka (The laborer and the man with the white hand 88; The toiler and the lazy man 4; The worker and the man with the white hands 90; The working man and the man with the white hands 89; The workman and the man with white hands 91, 231)
Chertopkhanov and Nedopyuskin 65, 102 [Chertopkhanov i Nedopyuskin]
Chertopkhanov i Nedopyuskin (Chertopkhanov and Nedopyuskin 65, 102; Native oddities 95; Tchertop-Hanov and Nedopyuskin 3; Tchertopkhanoff and Nedopiuskin 4)
The children of the czar 241 [Burmistr]

[43]

Christ 88–91, 231 [Khristos]
Chto ya budu dumat? (What shall I think? 88–91)
* Chto za pogoda zlaya
Ch'ya vina? (Whose fault? 91)
Clara Militch 3, 4, 5, 24, 127 [Klara Milich]
A contented man 88–91 [Dovol'nyĭ chelovek]
A conversation 90, 91, 128, 231 [Razgovor]
A conversation on the highway 23 [Razgovor na bol'shoĭ doroge]
A correspondence 3–5, 129 [Perepiska]
The correspondent 4 [Korrespondent]
The counting-house 3, 4, 12, 65, 95, 252, 253 [Kontora]
The country 91, 130 [Derevnya]
The country doctor 95, 102 [Uyezdnyĭ lekar']
The country woman 23 [Provintzialka]
The cup 91 [Kubok]
A curse 91 [Proklyatiye]

* Daĭ mne ruku — i poĭdiom my v pole
A daughter of Russia 33 [Neschastnaya]
"Dear Mary" 202A [Masha]
Death 3, 4, 65, 102 [Smert']
* Ded
Derevnya (The country 91, 130; In the village 89, 231; The village 88, 90)
* Derevnya: stikhotvoreniye
"Desperate" 132 [Otchayannyĭ]
A desperate character 3, 7, 9, 12 [Otchayannyĭ]
The destruction of the world 88 [Konetz sveta]
A dialogue 88, 89 [Razgover]
The diary of a hunter 309 [Zapiski okhotnika]
Diary of a sportsman 346 [Zapiski okhotnika]
The diary of a superfluous man 3–5, 11, 20, 27, 367 [Dnevnik lishnevo cheloveka]
Dimitri Roudine 1, 2, 133 [Rudin]
The district doctor 3, 4, 12, 19, 65, 254–267 [Uyezdnyĭ lekar']
Dlya nedolgovo svidan'ya (Serenade 232)
* Dnevnik devochki S. Butkevich
Dnevnik lishnevo cheloveka (The diary of a superfluous man 3–5, 11, 20, 27, 367)
The dog 3–5, 88–91, 203–206 [Sobaka]
* Dolgiye belyye tuchi plyvut
Don Quixote and Hamlet 34 [Gamlet i Don-Kikhot]
Dost thou hearken to the words of the fool 88 [Uslyshish' sud gluptza]
The doves 88, 89, 91, 231 [Golubi]
Dovol'no. Otryvok iz zapisok umershevo khudozhnika (Enough 3; It is enough 4, 5)
Dovol'nyĭ chelovek (A contented man 88–91; A self-satisfied man 231)
The dream, 4, 5, 134 [Son]
Dream tales and prose poems 3
Drozd I; II (The blackbird 91)
* Drugaya noch'
The duellist 3 [Bretior]

Durak (The blockhead 88, 89, 200, 231; The fool 91, 208)
Dva bogacha (Two rich men 90, 91; Which is the richer? 89; Who is the richer 88, 231)
Dva brata (The two brothers 88–91, 231)
Dva chetverostishiya (Two four-line stanzas 4; The two poets 89; Two quatrains 88, 90, 231; Two stanzas 91, 225)
* Dva gusara L. N. Tolstovo
Dva pomeshchika (Two country gentlemen 3, 65; Two landed proprietors 4; Two landowners 102; The two village lords 95)
Dva priyatelya (The two friends 3–5, 110)
* Dva slova o Granovskom
* Dve sestry
Dvoryanskoye gnezdo (A house of gentlefolk 3, 10, 16, 64; Liza 1, 2, 68, 69, 320, 322, 330, 370; A nest of gentlefolk 22, 310, 311; A nest of the gentry 76; A nest of hereditary legislators 77; A nest of nobles 1, 190; A noble nest 2; A nobleman's nest 4, 5, 78)
Dying plea to Tolstoy 135 [Tolstomu, L. N.]
Dym (Smoke 1–5, 7–11, 97–100, 234, 317, 325, 327, 346; Life at Baden 97)

An eastern legend 91, 231 [Vostochnaya legenda]
An eastern tale 89, 90 [Vostochnaya legenda]
The egoist 88–91, 207, 231
* Ekspromt
The end of Chertopkhanov 3, 4, 6, 65, 102 [Konetz Chertopkhanova]
The end of the world 89–91, 231 [Konetz sveta]
Enemy and friend 4, 90, 231 [Vrag i drug]
Enough 3 [Dovol'no]
Ermolai and the miller's wife 95, 102 [Yermolaĭ i mel'nichikha]
The estate office 102 [Kontora]
Evening in the country 136 [Otkuda veyet tishinoĭ? . . .]
An evening in Sorrento 23 [Vecher v Sorrente]
An excursion to the forest belt 4, 5 [Poyezdka v Poles'ye]
The execution of Tropmann 18 [Kazn' Tropmana]
The experiences of a sportsman 95, 312 [Zapiski okhotnika]

The family charge 23 [Nakhlebnik]
Father Alexyei's story 3–5 [Rasskaz ottza Alekseya]
Fathers and children 4, 5, 10, 13, 16, 35 [Ottzy i deti]
Fathers and sons 1–3, 7–9, 11, 36–58, 137–139, 314, 316, 348, 395 [Ottzy i deti]
Faust; rasskaz v devyati pis'makh (Faust; a story in nine letters 3–5, 140, 141)
* Faust, tragediya. Soch. Giote. Perevod M. Vronchenko

TITLE INDEX

The feast of the supreme being 90 [Pir u verkhovnovo sushchestva]
Fedya (Freddy 151)
The fields of the blest 89 [Lazurnoye tzarstvo]
* Filippo Strodzi
A fire at sea 142–145, *564* [Pozhar na more]
First love 3, 4, 5, 11, 14, 15, 22, 24, 27, 28, 59–61, 146–150, *312, 313* [Pervaya lyubov']
Foma the bireouk 95 [Biryuk]
Foma, the wolf 12, 268 [Biryuk]
The fool 91, 208 [Durak]
The fool's judgment thou wilt hear 89 [Uslyshish' sud gluptza]
The forest and the steppe 3, 4, 65, 86, 95, 102 [Les i step']
Fraza (Phrases 91)
Freddy 151 [Fedya]
The freeholder Ovsyanikov 4, 65 [Odnodvoretz Ovsyannikov]
Friend and enemy 88, 91 [Vrag i drug]
Friend and foe 89 [Vrag i drug]
The funeral 95 [Kas'yan a Krasivoï Mechi]

Gad (A snake 91)
Gamlet i Don-Kikhot (Don Quixote and Hamlet 34; Hamlet and Don Quixote 62, 63, 153–156, *460*)
Gamlet Shchigrovskovo uyezda (The Hamlet of the Shtchigri district 3, 4, 65; The higher provincial society 95; Prince Hamlet of Shchigrovo 102)
Gde tonko, tam i rviotsya (One may spin a thread too finely 198; Where it is thin, there it breaks 23)
* General-poruchik Patkul'; tragediya v pyati deĭstviyakh v stikhakh. Soch. Nestora Kukol'nikova
Ghosts 152 [Prizraki]
Gogol, Zhukovsky, Krylov, Lermontov, Zagoskin 18
Golubi (The doves 88, 89, 91, 231; Two doves 90)
* Grafinya Donato
* Groza
Groza promchalas' (The storm has passed 294)

Hamlet and Don Quixote 62, 63, 153–156, *460* [Gamlet i Don-Kikhot]
Hamlet of Shshtchigry county 4 [Gamlet Shchigrovskovo uyezda]
The Hamlet of the Shtchigri district 3, 65 [Gamlet Shchigrovskovo uyezda]
Hang him! 88–91, 231 [Povesit' yevo!]
A hapless girl 4, 5 [Neschastnaya]
The happy land 88, 231 [Lazurnoye tzarstvo]
The higher provincial society 95 [Gamlet Shchigrovskovo uyezda]
History of a town, ed M. E. Saltykoff [Review] 229

Hor and Kalinitch 3, 269 [Khor' i Kalinych]
The hour glass 91 [Pesochnyye chasy]
A house of gentlefolk 3, 10, 16, 64 [Dvoryanskoye gnezdo]
How beautiful were once the roses 209 [Kak khoroshi, kak svezhi byli rozy]
How fair, how fresh were the roses 91 [Kak khoroshi, kak svezhi byli rozy]
How lovely and fresh those roses were! 88 [Kak khoroshi, kak svezhi byli rozy]
"How lovely, how fresh were the roses . . ." 90 [Kak khoroshi, kak svezhi byli rozy]
How a Russian dies 95 [Smert']
How Russians meet death 270 [Smert']
How were the roses so fresh and so fair? 89 [Kak khoroshi, kak svezhi byli rozy]
A hunter's sketches 65 [Zapiski okhotnika]

I feel pity 91 [Mne zhal']
I rose from my bed at night 91 [Ya vstal noch'yu]
I walked amid high mountains 91 [Ya shel sredi vysokikh gor]
I wander round the lake 157 [Brozhu nad ozerom . . . tumanny]
The idiot 158 [Strannaya istoriya]
In front of the guillotine 159 [Kazn' Tropmana]
In memoriam 89 [Pamyati Yu. P. Vrevskoï]
In memory of I.P.W. 88 [Pamyati Yu. P. Vrevskoï]
In Memory of J. P. Vrevsky 4 [Pamyati Yu. P. Vrevskoï]
In the village 89, 231 [Derevnya]
The inn 3–5 [Postoyalyĭ dvor]
The insect 88–91, 231 [Nasekomoye]
Instead of an introduction 18
* Irodiada (Gustava Flobera)
* Iskusheniye svyatovo Antoniya
* Ispoved'
Istina i pravda (Truth and justice 91)
Istoriya leĭtenanta Yergunova (Lieutenant Yergunov's story 3; The story of Lieutenant Ergunoff 4, 5; Strange adventure of Lieutenant Yergunof)
It is enough 4, 5 [Dovol'no]
* Iz pis'ma v redaktziyu "Vestnika Yevropy" po povodu smerti S. K. Bryullovoï
* Iz poemy, predannoĭ sozhzheniyu
* Iz-za granitzy. Pis'mo pervoye

The Jew 3–5, 8, 9, 17 [Zhid]
The journalist 90 [Korrespondent]
Jupiter's feast 89 [Pir u verkhovnovo sushchestva]

* K . . . (Cherez polya k kholmam . . .)
K*** To ne lastochka . . . (To*** It is not the twittering swallow . . . 91)
* K. A. Farngagenu fon Enze
* K. A. S.

* K chemu tverzhu ya stikh unylyĭ
* K Venere Meditzeĭskoĭ
Kak khoroshi, kak svezhi byli rozy (How beautiful were once the roses etc 88–91, 209, 231)
Kamen' (The stone 88–91, 231)
Karataeff 95 [Piotr Petrovich Karatayev]
Kassyan of Fair Springs 3, 21, 65, 102 [Kas'yan s Krasivoĭ Mechi]
Kasyan from the Fair-Metcha 4 [Kas'yan s Krasivoĭ Mechi]
Kas'yan s Krasivoĭ Mechi (The funeral 95; Kassyan of Fair Springs 3, 21, 65, 102; Kasyan from the Fair-Metcha 4)
Kazn' Tropmana (The execution of Tropmann 18; In front of the guillotine 159)
Kholostyak (The bachelor 23, 31)
Khor' i Kalinych (Hor and Kalinitch 3, 269; Khor and Kalinich 4, 65, 95, 102)
Khristos (Christ 88–91, 231)
King Lear of the Russian steppes 4, 5, 160–162 [Stepnoĭ korol' Lir]
The kiss 163, 299 [Potzeluĭ]
Klara Milich 3, 4, 5, 24, 127 (After death 116)
Knock, knock, knock 3–5, 24 [Stuk . . . Stuk . . . Stuk!]
The knocking 102 [Stuchit]
* Kogda davno zabytoye nazvan'ye
Kogda menya ne budet (When I am no more 91)
Kogda s toboĭ rasstalsya ya (When I from thee was forced to part 307)
* Kogda ya molyus'
Kogda ya odin . . . Dvoĭnik (When I am alone . . . The double 91)
* Konetz
Konetz Chertopkhanova (The end of Chertopkhanov 3, 4, 6, 65, 102; Makel-Adel 178, 179)
Konetz sveta (The destruction of the world 88; The end of the world 89–91, 231)
* Konetz zhizni
Kontora (The counting-house 3, 4, 12, 65, 95, 252, 253; The estate office 102)
Korrespondent (The correspondent 4; The journalist 90; The newspaper correspondent 88, 231; The reporter 89, 91)
Krilof and his fables 164
* Kroket v Vindzore
* Krotkiye l'yutsya luchi
Kubok (The cup 91)
Kuropatki (The partridges 91)

The laborer and the man with the white hand 88 [Chernorabochiĭ i beloruchka]
The lady from the provinces 165 [Provintzialka]
The last good-bye 89 [Posledneye svidaniye]
The last meeting 88, 90, 91 [Posledneye svidaniye]

Lazurnoye tzarstvo (The azure realm 4; The fields of the blest 89; The happy land 88, 231; The realm of azure 90, 91)
A Lear of the steppes 1, 3, 22, 166–171 [Stepnoĭ korol' Lir]
Lebediana 95 [Lebedyan']
Lebedyan' 3, 4, 65, 102 (Lebediana 95)
* Legenda o sv. Yuliane Milostivom (Gustava Flobera)
Les i step' (Forest and steppe 3, 4, 65, 86, 95, 102)
* Lesnaya tish'
Let's keep a good heart 88 [My yeshche povoyuyem!]
Letters 66, 67,135, 172–177
L'gov 3, 4, 65, 95, 102 (Nothing like Russian leather 243)
Lieutenant Yergunov's story 3 [Istoriya leĭtenanta Yergunova]
Life at Baden 97 [Dym]
A literary party at P. A. Pletnyov's 18 [Literaturnyĭ vecher u P. A. Pletniova]
Literary reminiscences and autobiographical fragments 18 [Literaturnyye i zhiteĭskiye vospominaniya]
Literaturnyĭ vecher u P. A. Pletniova (A literary party at P. A. Pletnyov's 18)
Literaturnyye i zhiteĭskiye vospominaniya (Literary reminiscences and autobiographical fragments 18)
The live relic 102 [Zhivyye moshchi]
Living holy relics 4 [Zhivyye moshchi]
The living mummy 271 [Zhivyye moshchi]
A living relic 3, 12, 24, 65, 272–276 [Zhivyye moshchi]
Liza 1, 2, 68, 69, 320, 322, 330, 370 [Dvoryanskoye gnezdo]
Love 91 [Lyubov']
Lyubov' (Love 91)

Makel-Adel 178, 179 [Konetz Chertopkhanova]
Malinovaya voda (Raspberry spring 3, 65; Raspberry water 4, 95, 102, 277)
The man in the grey spectacles 18 [Chelovek v serykh ochkakh]
Masha 3, 4, 88–91, 231 (Dear Mary 202A)
A meeting 91 [Vstrecha]
Memoirs of a sportsman 4, 5 [Zapiski okhotnika]
The memory of U. P. Vrevskaya 90 [Pamyati Yu. P. Vrevskoĭ]
Mesyatz v derevne (A month in the country 23, 25, 26, 70–73, 181–183, 549)
Milostynya (Alms 88, 89, 91, 231; Charity 90)
Mne zhal' (I feel pity 91)
Moi derev'ya (My trees 91)
Moĭ sosed Radilov (My neighbour Radilov 3, 4, 65, 95, 102)
Molitva (Prayer 88–91, 212, 231)
Monakh (The monk 88–91, 231)

TITLE INDEX

The monk 88–91, 231 [Monakh]
Monsieur François 180 [Chelovek v serykh ochkakh]
A month in the country 23, 25, 26, 70–73, 181–183, 549 [Mesyatz v derevne]
Moomoo 19, 184 [Mumu]
More children of the Czar 242 [Piotr Petrovich Karatayev]
Morskoye plavaniye (On the sea 89, 91; A sea voyage 4, 90, 231; A trip by sea 88)
Mou-Mou 185 [Mumu]
Mumu 3–5, 17, 20, 21, 24, 74, 75, 186–189, 367 (Moomoo 19, 184; Mou-Mou 185)
The museum 299 [Muzeĭ]
Muzeĭ (The museum 299)
My adversary 89, 91 [Sopernik]
My dog 231 [Sobaka]
My mates sent me! 18 [Nashi poslali]
My neighbour Radilov 3, 4, 65, 95, 102 [Moĭ sosed Radilov]
My opponent 88 [Sopernik]
My trees 91 [Moi derev'ya]
My yeshche povoyuyem (Let's keep a good heart 88; We are still at war 89; We shall still fight on 4; We'll still go on fighting 90; We will still fight on 91; We will struggle 231)

N. N. 88–90 (To N. N. 91)
* Na Al'banskikh gorakh chto za d'yavol takoĭ?
* Na Druzhinina
* Na Ketchera
* Na Kudryavtzeva
* Na Nikitenko
* Na okhote letom
* Na zare
Nakanune (On the eve 1, 3–5, 10, 11, 79–85, 312, 313, 324)
Nakhlebnik (The family charge 23; A poor gentleman 25, 26)
Nasekomoye (The insect 88–91, 231)
Nashi poslali (My mates sent me! 18)
Native oddities 95 [Chertopkhanov i Nedopyuskin]
Nature 89–91, 210, 231 [Priroda]
* Ne zhdiote l' vy, chto nazovu ya
Necessitas, Vis, Libertas 88–91
Neostorozhnost' (Carelessness 23)
Neschastnaya (A daughter of Russia 33; A hapless girl 4, 5; The unfortunate one 111; An unfortunate woman 29; An unhappy girl 3, 8, 9)
* Neskol'ko slov o novoĭ komedii g. Ostrovskovo "Bednaya nevesta"
* Neskol'ko slov ob opere Meiyerbera "Prorok"
* Neskol'ko slov a stikhotvoreniyakh F. I. Tyutcheva
* Neskol'ko slov o Zhorzh Sand
* Neskol'ko zamechaniĭ o russkom khozyaĭstve i o russkom krest'yanine

Nessun maggior dolore 91
A nest of gentlefolk 22, 310, 311 [Dvoryanskoye gnezdo]
A nest of the gentry 76 [Dvoryanskoye gnezdo]
A nest of hereditary legislators 77 [Dvoryanskoye gnezdo]
A nest of nobles 1, 190 [Dvoryanskoye gnezdo]
* Neva
New poems in prose 191 [Novyye stikhotvoreniya v proze]
The newspaper correspondent 88, 231 [Korrespondent]
* Nikolaĭ Ivanovich Turgenev
Nimfy (The nymphs 88–91, 211, 231)
Nishchiĭ (The beggar 88–91, 231)
A noble nest 2 [Dvoryanskoye gnezdo]
The nobleman of the steppe 192 [Stepnoĭ korol' Lir]
A nobleman's nest 4, 5, 78 [Dvoryanskoye gnezdo]
* Noch' i den'
Nothing like Russian leather 243 [L'gov]
Nov' (Virgin soil 1–6, 10, 112–114, 335, 337, 340, 343, 346, 563)
Novyye stikhotvoreniya v proze (New poems in prose 191)
* Novyye pis'ma Pushkina
The nymphs 88–91, 211, 231 [Nimfy]

O moya molodost'! O moya svezhest'! (Oh my youth! 91)
* O prichinakh razryva s "Sovremennikom"
O solov' yakh (About nightingales 18)
* O stikhotvoreniyakh Ya. P. Polonskovo
* O vykhode v svet Fausta Giote v perevode M. Vronchenko
* O yubileye Krashevskovo
* O "Zapiskakh ruzheĭnovo okhotnika" S. T. Aksakova
* Ob Arture Benni
* Obed v obshchestve angliĭskovo Literaturnovo fonda
* Ocherki i rasskazy L. Kladelya
* Odin, opyat' odin
The Odnodvoretz 95 [Odnodvoretz Ovsyannikov]
Odnodvoretz Ovsyannikov (The freeholder Ovsyanikov 4, 65; The Odnovoretz 95; Ovsyanikov, the freeholder 102; The peasant proprietor Ovsyanikov 3)
Oh my youth! 91 [O moya molodost'!]
Old age 231 [Starik]
The old man 88–91 [Starik]
Old portraits 3–5, 7, 9, 193, 194 [Staryye portrety]
The old woman 88–91, 231 [Starukha]
On arguing 91 [S kem sporit'?]
On the eve 1, 3–5, 10, 11, 79–85, 312, 313, 324 [Nakanune]
On the rack 91 [Popalsya pod koleso]

On the road 195–197 [V doroge; Variatzii III]
On the sea 89, 91 [Morskoye plavaniye]
One may spin a thread too finely 198 [Gde tonko, tam i rviotsya]
An Oriental legend 88 [Vostochnaya legenda]
Osen' (Autumn 121, 122)
* Osenniĭ vecher . . . Nebo yasno . . .
Otchayannyĭ ("Desperate" 132; A desperate character 3, 7, 9, 12; A reckless character 4, 5)
Otkrytiye pamyatnika A. S. Pushkinu v Moskve (What Pushkin merits from Russia 306)
Otkuda veyet tishinoĭ? . . . (Evening in the country 136)
Otryvki iz vospominaniĭ svoikh i chuzhikh (Sketches and reminiscences 233)
Ottzy i deti (Fathers and children 4, 5, 10, 13, 16, 35; Fathers and sons 1–3, 7–9, 11, 36–58, 137–139, *314–316, 348, 395*)
* Otvet "Inogorodnomu obyvatelyu"
Ovsyanikov, the freeholder 102 [Odnodvoretz Ovsyanikov]
* Ozhidaniye

* Pamyati A. V. Druzhinina
Pamyati Yu. P. Vrevskoĭ (In memoriam 89; In memory of I. P. W. 88; In memory of J. P. Vrevsky 4; The memory of U. P. Vrevskaya 90; To the memory of J. P. W-Skaja 231; To the memory of Yu. P. Vrevskaya 91)
* Parasha
* Parodiya na stikhotvoreniye A. A. Feta
A parting 299 [Proshchaniye]
The partridges 91 [Kuropatki]
The path to love 91 [Put' k lyubvi]
The peasant proprietor Ovsyanikov 3 [Odnodvoretz Ovsyanikov]
Pegas 18 [Pegaz]
Pegasus 86, 199 [Pegaz]
Pegaz (Pegas 18; Pegasus 86, 199)
* Pered okhotoĭ
* Pered sudom
Perepelka (The quail 18)
Perepiska (A correspondence 3–5, 129)
* Perevod "Demona" na angliĭski yazyk
* Perevod "Germanii" Geine na russki yazyk
* Perevod poemy Lermontova "Mtzyri"
Pergamos excavations 18 [Pergamskiye raskopki]
Pergamskiye raskopki (Pergamos excavations 18)
Pervaya lyubov' (First love 3–5, 11, 14, 15, 22, 24, 27, 28, 59–61, 146–150, *312, 313*)
* Pervyĭ sneg
Pesn' torzhestvuyushcheĭ lyubvi (The song of love triumphant 4, 235, 236; The song of triumphant love 3, 5, 101, 237, 238)
* Pesnya Klerkhen iz "Egmonta"
Pesochnyye chasy (The hour glass 91)

Petushkov 3–5, 8, 9, 12 (Vassilissa 300)
Pevtzy (A Russian singing-match 244; The singers 3, 4, 24, 65, 102, 282–287; The tavern 95)
Phantoms; a fantasy 3–5 [Prizraki]
Photographs from Russian life 240 [Zapiski okhotnika]
Phrases 91 (Fraza)
Piotr Petrovich Karatayev 3, 4, 65, 95, 102 (More children of the Czar 242)
Pir u verkhovnovo sushchestva (The banquet of the deity 231; The banquet of the supreme being 91; Beneficence and gratitude 124; Jupiter's feast 89; The supreme being's banquet 88; The supreme being's feast 4)
Pisatel' i kritik (Author and critic 91)
* Pis'ma, 1831–1883
* Pis'ma iz Berlina
* Pis'ma o franko-prusskoĭ voĭne
* Pis'ma k Ye. Ya. Kolbasinu
* Pis'ma iz poslaniya k A. A. Fetu
* Pis'mo k redaktoru gazety "Le XIX-e siecle" o romane L. N. Tolstovo "Voĭna i mir"
* Pis'mo k redaktoru po povodu smerti gr. A. K. Tolstovo
* Pis'mo slushatel'nitzam zhenskikh vrachebnykh kursov
* "Plemyannitza"; roman. Soch. Yevgeniĭ Tur
* Po povodu otklika Krayevskovo na "Vospominaniya o Belinskom"
Po povodu "Ottzov i deteĭ" (Apropos of "Fathers and Children" 18, 118)
* Po povodu perevoda "Zapisok okhotnika" na frantzuzski yazyk
Poems in prose 3–5, 87–91 [Stikhotvoreniya v proze] *See also* individual titles, 200–226
* Poeticheskiye eskizy. Al'manakh stikhotvoreniĭ
* Pokazaniya po delu "O 32-kh litzakh, obvinyayemykh v snosheniyakh s londonskimi propagandistami"
* Pokhishcheniye
Pokhozhdeniya podporuchika Bubnova (The adventure of second lieutenant Bubnov 115)
* Pomeshchik
A poor gentleman 25, 26 [Nakhlebnik]
Popalsya pod koleso (On the rack 91)
Porog'; son (The threshold 90, 91, 219–222)
Poseshcheniye (A visit 88–91, 226)
Posle smerti *See* Klara Milich
Poslednye svidaniye (The last good-bye 89; The last meeting 88, 90, 91)
* Poslednyaya stzena pervoĭ chasti "Fausta" Giote
Postoyalyĭ dvor (The inn 3–5)
Potzeluĭ (The kiss 163, 299)
Povesit' yevo! (Hang him! 88–91, 231)
* Povesti, skazki i rasskazy Kazaka Luganskovo
Poyezdka v Al'bano i Fraskati (A trip to Albano and Frascati 18)

TITLE INDEX 49

Poyezdka v Poles'ye (An excursion to the forest belt 45; A tour in the forest 3)
Pozhar na more (A fire at sea 142–145, 564)
Prayer 88–91, 212, 231 [Molitva]
* Predisloviye k izdaniyu "Povesteĭ i rasskazov
* Predisloviye k izdaniyu sochineniĭ 1874 g.
* Predisloviye k otdel'nomu izdaniyu "Dyma"
* Predisloviye k Sobraniyu romanov v izdaniĭ 1880 g.
The priest's son 227 [Rasskaz ottza Alekseya]
Prince Hamlet of Shchigrovo 102 [Gamlet Shchigrovskovo uyezda]
Priroda (Nature 89–91, 210, 231)
Prizraki (Ghosts 152; Phantoms 3–5; Specters 239; Visions 301–303)
* Prizvaniye
Proklyatiye (A curse 91)
Proshchaniye (A parting 299)
* Prosper Merime
Prostota (Simplicity 91)
The provincial lady 25, 26, 92 [Provintzialka]
The provincial woman, and her nephew the artist 95 [Tat'yana Borisovna i yeio plemyannik]
Provintzialka (The country woman 23; The lady from the provinces 165; The provincial lady 25, 26, 92)
* Proyekt programmy "Obshchestva dlya rasprostraneniya gramotnosti i nachal'novo obrazovaniya"
Punin i Baburin 3, 4, 5, 7, 9, 14, 93
Put' k lyubvi (The path to love 91)
* Pyat'desyat nedostatkov ruzheĭnovo okhotnika i pyat'desyat nedostatkov lyagavoĭ sobaki
Pyetushkov 3–5, 8, 9, 12 [Petushkov]
Pyotr Petrovich Karataev 65, 102 [Piotr Petrovich Karatayev]

The quail 18 [Perepelka]
A quiet backwater 3, 22, 228 [Zatish'ye]
A quiet spot 11 [Zatish'ye]

Raspberry spring 3, 65 [Malinovaya voda]
Raspberry water 4, 95, 102, 277 [Malinovaya voda]
* Rasskaz I. Ya. Pavlovskovo "En cellule. Impressions d'un nihiliste"
Rasskaz attza Alekseya (Father Alexyei's story 3–5; The priest's son 227)
The rattling 4 [Stuchit!]
The rattling of wheels 3, 65 [Stuchit]
* Razgadka
Razgovor (A conversation 90, 91, 128, 231; A dialogue 88, 89)
* Razgovor; stikhotvoreniye
Razgovor na bol'shoĭ doroge (A conversation on the highway 23)
* Razluka
The realm of azure 90, 91 [Lazurnoye tzarstvo]

* Rech', proiznesennaya v Moskve 6 marta 1879 g
A reckless character 4, 5 [Otchayannyĭ]
The region of dead calm 4, 5 [Zatish'ye]
Reminiscences of Belinsky 18 [Vospominaniya o Belinskom]
The rendezvous 102, 278–281 [Svidaniye]
The reporter 89, 91 [Korrespondent]
* Rimskaya èlegiya
The rival 4, 90 [Sopernik]
* Roman B. Auerbakha "Dacha na Reine"
* Roman M. Dyukana "Utrachennyye sily"
The rose 88–91, 231 [Roza]
"The roses were lovely, the roses were fresh ..." 231 [Kak khoroshi, kak svezhi bylirozy]
Roza (Rose 88–91, 231)
Rudin 3–5, 11, 13, 15 (Dimitri Roudine 1, 2, 133)
The ruffian 94 [Bretior]
A rule of life 89, 91, 213, 231 [Zhiteĭskoye pravilo]
The Russian language 88–90, 214, 231 [Russki yazyk]
Russian life in the interior; or, The experiences of a sportsman 95, 312 [Zapiski okhotnika]
A Russian singing-match 244 [Pevtzy]
A Russian sorcerer 230 [Strannaya istoriya]
The Russian tongue 91, 215, 216 [Russki yazyk]
* Russki
Russki yazyk (The Russian language 88–90, 214, 231; The Russian tongue 91, 215, 216)

S kem sporit'? (On arguing 91)
* Sadovnik
* Satira na mal'chika-vseznaĭku
A sea voyage 4, 90, 231 [Morskoye plavaniye]
A self-satisfied man 231 [Dovol'nyĭ chelovek]
Senilia 96, 231 [Stikhotvoreniya v proze]
Serenade 232 [Dlya nedolgovo svidan'ya]
Sfinks (The sphinx 88–91, 231)
Shchi (Cabbage-soup 88–91, 201, 202, 231)
Simplicity 91 [Prostota]
The singers 3, 4, 24, 65, 102, 282–287 [Pevtzy]
Sinitza (The wood lark 308)
Sketches and reminiscences 233 [Otryvki iz vospominaniĭ svoikh i chuzhikh]
The skulls 88–91, 231 [Cherepa]
* Slobozhane; malorossiĭskiye rasskazy Grigoriya Danilevskovo
Smert' (Death 3, 4, 65, 102; How a Russian dies 95; How Russians meet death 270)
* "Smert' Lyapunova"; drama v pyati deĭstviyakh v proze. Soch. S. A. Gedeonova
Smoke 1–5, 7–11, 97–100, 234, 317, 325, 327, 346 [Dym]
A snake 91 [Gad]
Sobaka (The dog 3–5, 88–91, 203–206; My dog 231; Treasure 224)
Son (The dream 4, 5, 134)

The song of love triumphant 4, 235, 236 [Pesn' torzhestvuyushcheĭ lyubvi]
The song of triumphant love 3, 5, 101, 237, 238 [Pesn' torzhestvuyushcheĭ lyubvi]
Sopernik (The adversary 231; My adversary 89, 91; My opponent 88; The rival 4, 90)
* Sovremennyye zametki
The sparrow 88–91, 217, 218, 231 [Vorobeĭ]
Specters 239 [Prizraki]
The sphinx 89–91, 231 [Sfinks]
A sportsman's notebook 102–104 [Zapiski okhotnika]
A sportsman's sketches 3, 105, 476 [Zapiski okhotnika]
Spring floods 1, 106, 293, 326, 328 [Veshniye vody]
Spring freshets 4, 5 [Veshniye vody]
Spring torrents 28, 562 [Veshniye vody]
Starik (Old age 231; The old man 88–91)
Starukha (The old woman 88–91, 231)
* Staryĭ pomeshchik
Staryye portrety (Old portraits 3–5, 7, 9, 193, 194)
Stay! 90–91 (Stoĭ!]
* Steno
Stepnoĭ korol' Lir (King Lear of the Russian steppes 4, 5, 160–162; A Lear of the steppes 1, 3, 22, 166–171; The nobleman of the steppe 192)
The steward 165 [Burmistr]
Stikhotvoreniya v proze (New poems in prose 191; Poems in prose 3–5, 87–91; Senilia 96, 231) See also individual titles, 200–226
Stoĭ (Abide 89; Stay 90–91; Stop 88)
The stone 88–91, 231 [Kamen']
Stop! 88 [Stoĭ]
The storm has passed 294 [Groza promchalas']
The story of Lieutenant Ergunoff 4, 5 [Istoriya leĭtenanta Yergunova]
Strange adventure of Lieutenant Yergunof 295 [Istoriya leĭtenanta Yergunova]
A strange story 3–5, 7, 9, 12, 296, 297 [Strannaya istoriya]
Strannaya istoriya (The idiot 158; A Russian sorcerer 230; A strange story 3–5, 7, 9, 12, 296, 297)
Stuchit (The knocking 102, The rattling 4; The rattling of wheels 3, 65)
Stuk . . . Stuk . . . Stuk! (Knock, knock, knock 3–5, 24)
The supreme being's feast 4 [Pir u verkhovnovo sushchestva]
The supreme being's banquet 88 [Pir u verkhovnovo sushchestva]
Svidaniye (The assignation 195; The rendezvous 102, 278–281; The tryst 3, 4, 65, 289, 290–291)

Tales from the Note-book of a sportsman 107 [Zapiski okhotnika]

Tatyana Borisovna and her nephew 3, 4, 65, 102, 288 [Tat'yana Borisovna i yeio plemyannik
Tat'yana Borisovna i yeio plemyannik (The provincial woman, and her nephew the artist 95; Tatyana Borisovna and her nephew 3, 4, 65, 102, 288)
The tavern 95 [Pevtzy]
Tchertop-Hanov and Nedopyuskin 3 [Chertopkanov i Nedopyuskin]
Tchertopkhanoff and Nedopiuskin [Chertopkhanov i Nedopyuskin]
Thou shalt hear the fool's judgment 91 [Uslyshish' sud gluptza]
Thou shalt hear the judgment of the dullard 4 [Uslyshish' sud gluptza]
Three meetings 3–5, 298 [Tri vstrechi]
Three portraits 3–5, 8, 9 [Tri portreta]
The threshold 90, 91, 219–222 [Porog; son]
* T'ma
To*** It is not the twittering swallow . . . 91 [K*** (To ne lastochka . . .)]
To the memory of J. P. W-Skaja 231 [Pamyati Yu. P. Vrevskoĭ]
To the memory of Yu. P. Vrevskaya 91 [Pamyati Yu. P. Vrevskoĭ]
To N. N. 91 [N. N.]
The toiler and the lazy man 4 [Chernorabochiĭ i beloruchka]
* Tolpa
Tolstoĭ 135, 175
Tolstomu, L. N. (Dying plea to Tolstoy 135)
To-morrow! To-morrow! 88–91, 223 [Zavtra, zavtra]
Torrents of spring 3, 108, 109 [Veshniye vody]
A tour in the forest 3 [Poyezdka v Poles'ye]
Treasure 224 [Sobaka]
Tri portreta (Three portraits 3–5, 8, 9)
Tri vstrechi (Three meetings 3, 5, 298)
* Triokhsotletiye so dnya rozhdeniya Shekspira
A trip to Albano and Frascati 18 [Poyezdka v Al'bano i Fraskati]
A trip by sea 88 [Morskoye plavaniye]
Truth and justice 91 [Istina i pravda]
The tryst 3, 4, 65, 289, 290, 291 [Svidaniye]
The twins 91 [Bliznetzy]
The two brothers 88–91, 231 [Dva brata]
Two country gentlemen 3, 65 [Dva pomeshchika]
Two doves 90 [Golubi]
Two four-line stanzas 4 [Dva chetverostishiya]
The two friends 3–5, 110 [Dva priyatelya]
Two landed proprietors 4 [Dva pomeshchika]
Two landowners 102 [Dva pomeshchika]
The two poets 89 [Dva chetverostishiya]
Two quatrains 88, 90, 231 [Dva chetverostishiya]
Two rich men 90, 91 [Dva bogacha]
Two stanzas 91, 225 [Dva chetverostishiya]
The two village lords 95 [Dva pomeshchika]

TITLE INDEX 51

Ty zaplakal (You wept 91)
* Tzvetok

* U-a . . . U-a . . . (A baby's cry 91)
* Ukrainskiye narodnyye rasskazy" Marka Vovchka
* Un roman du comte Tolstoi
The unfortunate one 111 [Neschastnaya]
An unfortunate woman 29 [Neschastnaya]
An unhappy girl 3, 8, 9 [Neschastnaya]
Uslyshish' sud gluptza (Accept the verdict of fools 231; Dost thou harken to the words of the fool 88; The fool's judgment thou wilt hear 89; Thou shalt hear the fool's judgment 91; Thou shalt hear the judgment of the dullard 4; You shall hear the judgment of the dullard 4; You shall hear the judgment of the fool 90)
Uyezdnyĭ lekar' (The country doctor 95, 102; The district doctor 3, 4, 12, 19, 65, 254–267)

* V. N. B.
* V al'bom M. P. Botkinoĭ
V doroge; Variatzii III (On the road 195–197)
* V noch' letnyuyu, kogda, trevozhnoĭ grusti polnyĭ . . .
* Variatzii
Vassilissa 300 [Petushkov]
* Vecher
Vecher v Sorrente (An evening in Sorrento 23)
* Vesenniĭ vecher
Veshniye vody (Spring floods 1, 106, 293, 326, 328; Spring freshets 4, 5; Spring torrents 28, 562; Torrents of spring 3, 108, 109)
* Vil'gel'm Tell'; dramaticheskoye predstavleniye. Soch. Shillera. Perevod F. Millera
The village 88–90 [Derevnya]
The Vintage Turgenev 11
Virgin soil 1–6, 10, 112–114, 335, 337, 340, 343, 346, 563 [Nov']
Visions 301–303 [Prizraki]
A visit 88–91, 226 [Poseshcheniye]
* Vmesto vstupleniya
* Volshebnyye skazki Perro
Vorobeĭ (The sparrow 88–91, 217, 218, 231)
Vospominaniya o Belinskom (Reminiscences of Belinsky 18)
* Vospominaniya o Shevchenko
Vostochnaya legenda (An eastern legend 91, 231; An eastern tale 89, 90; An Oriental legend 88)
Vrag i drug (Enemy and friend 4, 90, 231; Friend and enemy 88, 91; Friend and foe 89)
Vstrecha (A meeting 91)
* Vstrecha moya s Belinskim

The watch 3–5, 304, 305 [Chasy]
We are still at war 89 [My yeshche povoyuyem]
We shall still fight on! 4 [My yeshche povoyuyem]
We will still fight on! 91 [My yeshche povoyuyem]
We will struggle 231 [My yeshche povoyuyem]
We'll still go on fighting! 90 [My yeshche povoyuyem]
What Pushkin merits from Russia 306 [Otkrytiye pamyatnika A. S. Pushkin v Moskve]
What shall I think? 88–91 [Chto ya budu dumat'?]
When I am alone . . . The double 91 [Kogda ya odin . . . Dvoĭnik]
When I am no more 91 [Kogda menya ne budet]
When I from thee was forced to part 307 [Kogda s toboĭ rasstalsya ya]
Where it is thin, there it breaks 23 [Gde tonko, tam i rviotsya]
Which is the richer? 89 [Dva bogacha]
Who is the richer? 88, 231 [Dva bogacha]
Whose fault? 91 [Ch'ya vina?]
The wolf 4 [Biryuk]
The wood lark 308 [Sinitza]
The worker and the man with white hands 90 [Chernorabochiĭ i beloruchka]
The working man and the man with the white hands 89 [Chernorabochiĭ i beloruchka]
The workman and the man with white hands 91, 231 [Chernorabochiĭ i beloruchka]
Worldly wisdom 90 [Zhiteĭskoye pravilo]

Ya shel sredi vysokikh gor (I walked amid high mountains 91)
* Ya vskhodil na kholm zelionyĭ
Ya vstal noch'yu (I rose from my bed at night 91)
Yakoff Pasynkoff 3–5
Yermolaĭ and the miller's wife 3, 4, 12, 65, 292 [Yermolaĭ i mel'nichikha]
Yermolaĭ i mel'nichikha (Ermolai and the miller's wife 95, 102; Yermolaĭ and the miller's wife 3, 4, 12, 65, 292)
You shall hear the judgment of the fool 90 [Uslyshish' sud gluptza]
You wept 91 [Ty zaplakal]

* Zagublennaya zhizn'
* Zametila li ty, o drug moĭ molchalivyĭ
* Zametka o M. M. Antokol'skom
* Zapiska ob izdanii zhurnala "Khozyaĭstvennyĭ ukazatel'
* Zapiska o N. V. Stankeviche
Zapiski okhotnika (Annals of a sportsman 1; The diary of a hunter 309; Diary of a sports-

Zapiski okhotnika, continued

man *346*; A hunter's sketches 65; Memoirs of a sportsman 4, 5; Photographs from Russian life 240; Russian life in the interior, or, The experiences of a sportsman 95, *312*; A sportsman's notebook 102–104; A sportsman's sketches 3, 105, *476*; Tales from the notebook of a sportsman 107) *See also* individual titles, 240–292

* Zapiski ruzheĭnovo okhotnika Orenburgskoĭ gubernii S. A. Aksakova

Zatish'ye (The antchar 117; A quiet backwater 3, 22, 228: A quiet spot 11; The region of dead calm 4, 5)

Zavtra, zavtra (To-morrow! To-morrow! 88–91, 223)

Zavtrak u predvoditelya (An amicable settlement 23)

Zhid (The Jew 3–5, 8, 9, 17)

Zhiteĭskoye pravilo (An axiom 88; A rule of life 89, 91, 213, 231; Worldly wisdom 90)

Zhivvye moshchi (A living relic etc 3, 4, 12, 24, 65, 102, 271–276)

Author and Translator Index

Abbott, Franklin Pierce, tr 1, 30
Abbott, Lawrence F. 484
Adams, Charlotte 368
Allen, W. H. 377
Annan, Noel 524
Anthony, Augustus M. 127
Apresyan, Stepan, tr 85
Arnold, Ethel M., tr 66

Balzac, Honoré de 421
Baring, Maurice 435, 436, 449
Barker, A. R. R. 356
Belgrave, Michael 72
Bennett, Arnold 413, 454, 489
Benton, Joel 381
Berlin, Isaiah 564; tr 15, 61
Bernstein, Edward 505
Bernstein, Herman, tr 219, 278
Bertensson, Sergeï 574
Bôcher, F. 378
Boyersen, Hjalmar Hjorth 331, 338, 350, 358, 397; tr 192
Brandes, Georg 385, 386, 412
Brewster, Dorothy 552
Brodianski, Nina 550
Brown, Alec, tr 15
Browne, William Hand, tr 1
Brückner, Alexander 434
Bryner, Cyril 568
Budberg, Moura, tr 81, 82
Burton, Reginald George 401
Butts, Sophie Michell 1

Cargill, Oscar 559
Carr, Edward Hallet 495, 497
Cecil, Lord David 15, 61, 537, 539
Chamberlin, William Henry 528
Chamot, Alfred Edward, tr 120
Child, T. E. 341
Chyzhevs'kyĭ, Dmytro 555
Clutton-Brock, Arthur 463
Colum, Padraic 452
Conrad, Joseph 27, 465, 466
Copeland, Charles Townsend 274
Cores, Lucy Michaella 44
Coulson, Jessie, tr 22
Cournos, John 135, 155, 448; tr 255
Courtney, William Leonard 424
Covan, Jenny, tr 165
Crawford, Virginia M. 410
Crossfield, H. 431
Curle, Richard H. P. 439

Daudet, Alphonse 362
Davis, F. M., tr 64, 68, 77
Dilke, Ashton Wentworth, tr 112, 343
Dillmann, A. C. 323

Dole, Nathan Haskell 391, 398; tr 150, 375
Domb, Jessie, tr 74
Duddington, Natalie, tr 100
Dupuy, Ernest 375
Durdik, Pavel, tr 153

Eastman, S. C., tr 385, 386, 412
Edmonds, Jane Loring, tr 379
Ettlinger, Amrei 530
Evans, Noel, tr 110

Fenn, Elisaveta, tr 71
Flaubert, Gustave 66, 496
Folejewski, Zbigniew 545
Foord, Edward, tr 296
Footman, David 547
Forbes, Nevill 86, 444
Ford, Ford Madox 441, 508–510
Ford, Marian 101
Freeborn, Richard 580

Galsworthy, John 487
Gardiner, Fanny Hale, tr 388
Gardiner, Gilbert, tr 83, 84
Garnett, Constance, tr 3, 10, 16, 25–27, 32, 37, 41, 43–45, 47, 50, 51, 57, 68, 91, 105, 114, 125, 146, 150, 167–171, 184, 186, 188, 193, 236, 247–249, 252, 259, 261, 265, 276, 284, 289, 290, 292
Garnett, David 25, 549
Garnett, Edward 3, 455
Gershenzon, Mikhail Osipovich 477
Gersoni, Henry, tr 20, 29, 367
Gettmann, Royal Alfred 321, 516
Gifford, Henry 541
Gilman, Richard 575
Gladstone, Joan M. 530
Gorchakov, O. 65; tr 60
Gosse, Edmund 491
Gough, Magaret, tr 198
Goy, E. D. 567
Gribble, Francis 438
Guerney, Bernard Guilbert, 137, 176; tr 58, 163

Halperin, George 525
Halperine-Kaminsky, Ely 66, 174
Hamilton, Lady George, tr 270
Hanna, George H. 85
Hapgood, Isabel Florence 376, 419; tr 4, 5, 134, 211, 235
Hare, Richard 532, 576; tr 13, 35, 78, 80
Harris, Frank 478
Hemmings, F. W. J. 542
Hepburn, Charles, tr 102–104
Hepburn, Natasha, tr 102–104
Hershkowitz, Harry 502

[53]

Hindus, Milton 579
Hodgetts, Edward Arthur Brayley 402
Hogarth, C. J., tr 39, 52
Howe, Irving 561
Howells, William D. 327, 330, 399, 400, 408, 445
Huneker, James Gibbons 422, 423

Isaacs, Bernard, tr 46, 76

James, Henry 4, 27, 332, 337, 365, 456, 535, 563
Jerrold, Maud F., tr 122, 157, 195
Jerrold, Sidney, tr 14
Johnston, Charles 390

Kappler, Richard George 581
Katscher, Leopold 392
Katz, M., tr 62
Kaun, Alexander 475, 504
Kazin, Alfred 554
Kelley, Cornelia Palsifer 498
Kingsley, William L. 344
Kisch, Sir Cecil Hermann, tr 123, 196
Koussevitzky, Serge 11
Kral, Josef Jiri, tr 153
Kropotkin, Piotr Alekseyevich 426
Kunitz, Joshua 492

Larremore, Wilbur 366
Lavrin, Janko 486, 494, 518, 536, 553
Lazarus, Agnes, tr 298
Lednicki, Wacław 558
Lehrman, Edgar H., tr 67
Lerner, Daniel 517
Lewis, Sinclair 45
Litvinov, Ivy (Low), tr 28, 75
Litvinov, Tatiana, tr 28
Lloyd, John Arthur Thomas 442, 462, 519, 520
Lord, Elizabeth Brereton, tr 306
Lubbock, Percy 467
Lynd, Robert 461

Macmullen, S. J., tr 96
Magarshack, David 67, 551; tr 18, 24, 108, 109, 566
Maichel, Karol 573
Mais, Stuart P. B. 469
Makanowitzky, Barbara, tr 56
Malleson, Miles 31, 92
Mamoulian, Rouben 70
Mandel, Oscar 578
Mandell, Max Solomon, tr 23, 70, 182
Manning, Clarence A. 501
Martin, Clara Barnes 342, 347, 372
Martin, Mildred A. 560
Mather, J. B., tr 89
Matlaw, Ralph E. 562, 565, 572
Matthews, W. K., tr 197
Mazon, André 91

Meiklejohn, James D. 95
Melik, Peter 67
Mérimée, Prosper 27
Michell, Sophie, tr 293
Mills, A. S., tr 533, 534
Milne, Ewart 18
Mirsky, D. S. 481, 488, 540, 571
Monkhouse, Allan 396
Moore, George 383, 393, 421
Morfill, William Richard 371
Morgan, Charles 523, 544
Morison, Walter, tr 285, 297
Mortimer, Raymond 522
Moxom, Philip Stafford 446
Muchnic, Helen 11, 531
Muller, Herbert Joseph 47

Newmarch, Rosa Harriet, tr 173
New York Public Library 570
Nichols, Robert, tr 63
Niewiadomsky, Nicolas E. 511
Nikolaieff, Alexander Mikhailovich, tr 199
Norton, C. E. 315
Noyes, George Rapall, tr 181, 191

Olgin, Moissaye Joseph 464
Orel, Harold 556
Osborne, E. A. 503

Palliser, Bury, tr 160
Panin, Ivan 387
Pardo-Bazán, Emilia 388
Patrick, George Zinovei, tr 191
Perry, Thomas Sergeant 324, 325, 328, 333, 334, 340, 380, 445; tr 1
Phelps, Gilbert 557
Phelps, William Lyon 23, 443, 499
Philipson, Morris 18
Poggioli, Renato 548
Pollen, John 151; tr 202A, 214
Preston, Harriet Waters 382
Pritchett, Victor Sawdon 52, 512, 521, 526, 577

Radoff, Sarah F. 474
Radziwill, Catherine 500
Raffi, Aram 19
Ralston, W. R. S. 339, 357; tr 1, 68, 69, 158, 164
Reavey, George, tr 48, 54
Reed, John 98
Rees, Roger, tr 91
Rhys, Ernest 113
Richter, E., tr 106, 107
Ritchie, Anne Thackeray 429
Robinson, E. 309
Rolleston, T. W., tr 34
Rowland-Brown, Lilian 471

Safford, Mary J., tr 126
Sampson, George 442

Sands, E. R. 53
Sandwich, Humphry 460
Sawyer, H. A., tr 447
Sayler, Oliver M. 473
Schimanskaya, Evgenia, tr 90
Schuyler, Eugene 326, 418; tr 1, 315
Schwartz, Delmore 50
Scott, George W., tr 33, 93
Seltzer, Thomas 37, 43
Sergievsky, Nicolas N. 529
Seznec, Jean 177
Shakhnovski 468
Shedden-Ralston, William Ralston, See Ralston, W. R. S.
Shepherd, Gertrude 404
Shevitch, S. E. 346
Shimanskaya, Yevgeniya Borisovna, See Schimanskaya
Shoenberg, Zlata, tr 74
Simmons, Ernest Joseph 18, 35
Slonim, Mark L'vovich 543, 553, 569
Snow, Francis Haffkine, tr 199
Snow, Valentine 527
Spector, Ivar 513–515, 551
Spooner, Walter Whipple, tr 127
Stanislavski, Konstantin Sergeyevich 479
Staratsky, G. V. 369
Stevens, Harry, tr 11
Stewart H., tr 299
Strauss, Walter A. 538
Strunsky, Simeon 432
Svyatopolk-Mirski, Dmitriĭ Petrovich, See Mirsky, D. S.
Swinnerton, Frank 490

Thanet, Octave 345
Thompson, A. R., tr 111
Tilley, Arthur 373
Todhunter, Maurice 403
Tolstaya, Aleksandra L'vovna 56
Tolstaya, Sof'ya Andreyevna (Bers) 506
Tolstoĭ, Il'ya 450
Tolstoy, See Tolstaya

Tomkeyeff, Serge, tr 468
Tonson, Jacob 437
Townsend, Rachelle S., tr 6, 113
Tsanoff, Radoslav Andrea 457
Tucker, Henry St George 453
Tuckerman, Bayard 363
Turner, Charles Edward 321, 352; tr 1, 79, 233

Underwood, E. G. 86
Underwood, Edna, tr 136, 308

Van Doren, Carl 38, 42
Varneke, Boris V. 546
Vogüe, Eugène Melchoir Marie de 379, 411, 447
Volkhovsky, Feliks Vadimovich 409
Volkonski, Sergeĭ Mikhaĭlovich 405–407

Waliszewski, Kazimierz 414–416
Wellek, René 552
West, William F., tr 1
Whibley, Charles 420
Wiener, Leo 138, 451, 480
Willcocks, Mary Patricia 472
Williams, Emlyn 71–73, 183
Williams, J. Evan, tr 305
Wilson, Edmund 18, 566
Winterich, John Tracy 51
Wisby, J. H., tr 226
Wischnewetsky, Florence K., tr 172
Woolf, Virginia 507

Yarmolinsky, Avrahm 11, 171, 193, 482, 483, 575, 575A

Zeitlin, Jacob 470
Zhitova, Varvara Nikolayevna 533, 534
Zimmern, Alice 348
Zimmern, Helen 348
Zola, Émile 66
Zubof, Roman I. 389

Recent Imprints NYPL

An Index to The Little Review 1914–1929. Compiled by Kenneth A. Lohf and Eugene P. Sheehy. 42 pages. $2.

There is a basis for the publisher's boast, on the dust jacket of *The Little Review Anthology*, that "No American magazine ever made as much literary history as *The Little Review* from 1914 to 1929." Subtitled "The Magazine that is Read by those who Write the Others," it is now read by those who pursue the careers of Joyce, Lewis (Wyndham), Pound, Crane (Hart), Williams, and . . . . (See our *Index* — which is, incidentally, an index to the *Anthology* as well as to the *Review*.)

George Gissing's Commonplace Book: A Manuscript in the Berg Collection of The New York Public Library. Edited, with an Introductory Essay, by Jacob Korg. 64 pages. $2.50.

The entries have been grouped under appropriate headings, following the precedent set by Gissing in his supposed editing of Ryecroft's diary: Philosophy and Opinion, Literature, Words, On the Times, Religion, Women, England, Lower Classes, Reviews, and Miscellaneous.

American Genealogical Periodicals: A Bibliography with a Chronological Finding-List. By Lester J. Cappon. 29 pages. $1.50.

"During the preparation of my paper, 'Genealogy, Handmaid of History,' I browsed in the files of a considerable number of genealogical magazines. . . . it occurred to me that a compilation of titles, with essential bibliographical information, might bring them into focus for the first time as a medium of information. . . . "

Emerson's American Lecture Engagements: A Chronological List. By William Charvat. 48 pages. $1.

Parthenia In-Violata or Mayden-Musicke for the Virginalls and Bass-Viol Selected by Robert Hole. Facsimile of the unique copy in The New York Public Library. Historical Introduction by Thurston Dart; with a Foreword by Sydney Beck and a Bibliographical Note by Richard J. Wolfe. 104 pages, clothbound. $9.

To Order: The Library pays postage and delivery charges. Orders amounting to less than $5 should be accompanied by check, stamps, or money order; larger orders will be billed.

Free on Request: *NYPL Publications in Print*, a 24-page list including a selection of titles available on microfilm.

Orders should be directed to the Public Relations Office, New York Public Library, Fifth Avenue and 42nd Street, New York 18, N. Y.